Skye Jethani sees the tragedy in divine commodification, but he does more than critique the darkness. He uses it as a mirror to help all of us find colonies of religious consumerism growing in our own hearts. And he uses the light of great saints and artists to lift our sights to something higher and deeper and wider than personal religious "customer satisfaction."

BRIAN MCLAREN, author/speaker (brianmclaren.net)

The Divine Commodity is a probing look at how the tentacles of consumerism have wrapped themselves around the American church, nearly choking it to spiritual death. Jethani manages to name the beast without condemning the many practitioners of consumer Christianity, and he speaks not only the hard word but also suggests ways that can help us break free.

MARK GALLI, Senior Managing Editor, *Christianity Today*
author, *Jesus Mean and Wild: The Unexpected Love of an Untamable God*

Salted with moments of delightful humor and fortified by sympathetic anecdotes and insights from the life and work of Vincent van Gogh, Skye Jethani's critique of a church without imagination is as persuasive as it is accessible and engaging.

PHYLLIS TICKLE, author, *The Great Emergence*

Jethani makes a compelling case that consumerism isn't simply a matter of Christians spending too much on themselves (which is true). Consumerism is a diabolic cancer that is subtley undermining the core values and practices of the kingdom. All American Christians need to read, discuss, and digest this book!

GREGORY A. BOYD, Senior Pastor, Woodland Hills Church
author, *The Myth of a Christian Nation*

Skye Jethani skillfully guides us in what it means to be faithful disciples in a culture that has literally sold its soul to the devil of consumerism. The *Divine Commodity* is a great antidote for the venomous spirit of our age.

ALAN HIRSCH, author of *The Forgotten Ways* and *reJesus*
a founder of shapevine.com

What an irony when the church turns the living God into a religious commodity, a cheap mirror of culture rather than a vivid reflection of God's revelation. Skye Jethani's winsome, artful, passionate, and compelling book is an antidote that can help undo this distortion and reopen our imaginations to the God who speaks true hope in Jesus Christ.

MARK LABBERTON, Senior Pastor, First Presbyterian Church of Berkeley
author, *The Dangerous Act of Worship*

Navigating American consumerism requires both the aptitude of a scholarly mind and the observational skills of a "culture junkie." Skye Jethani exhibits both in this book. With care, subtlety, cultural savvy, and theological acumen, he guides us through the consumerist maze that threatens Christian discipleship in our day. In so doing, he makes *The Divine Commodity* a primer for discerning a new Christian faithfulness amidst the market forces that so dominate American life today.

> DAVID FITCH, Reclaimingthemission.com
> Lindner Chair of Evangelical Theology, Northern Seminary
> author, *The Great Giveaway: Reclaiming the Mission of the Church from Big Business*

Even if it is doing so seductively and with a velvet glove, consumer capitalism is choking American evangelicalism to death. The church and real Christianity will survive, in various forms. But nothing short of the resuscitation of gospel imagination ... can now save evangelicalism. As vividly true and quietly brilliant as a van Gogh painting, Skye Jethani's book is an urgent, loving application of CPR. Evangelicals who read it may begin to breathe again.

> RODNEY CLAPP, author, *Border Crossings*

Skye artfully examines ways we have become McChurch in America. He boldly calls us to an alternate way of being without selling out to the consumer culture of our times.

> DAVE GIBBONS, author, *The Monkey and the Fish*

This book is a well-written diagnosis of what is seriously ailing the American church. If you want to address some of what is keeping us from being a positive influence in our society today, I highly recommend it. If you want to wake up in your bed tomorrow and go on believing everything is fine, DO NOT READ THIS BOOK!

> NEIL COLE, Director of Church Multiplication Associates
> author, *Organic Church, Cultivating a Life for God, Search & Rescue,* and *Organic Leadership*

Skye Jethani reflects on the Consumer Church and Consumer Christianity with incisive wit, wisdom, humility, humor, and prophetic insight. He juxtaposes the ideal of the "franchise" church with childlike faith, imaginative wonder, and nonconformist community, drawing on the examples of misfits like Vincent van Gogh and his art. Skye doesn't just talk about the imagination; he captures it.

> DR. RICK RICHARDSON, Associate Professor and Director of the Masters in Evangelism and Leadership, Wheaton College
> author, *Reimagining Evangelism* and *Evangelism Outside the Box*

DISCOVERING A FAITH BEYOND
CONSUMER CHRISTIANITY

THE
DIVINE
COMMODITY

SKYE JETHANI

ZONDERVAN

ZONDERVAN.com/
AUTHORTRACKER
follow your favorite authors

We want to hear from you. Please send your comments about this book to us in care of zreview@zondervan.com. Thank you.

The Divine Commodity
Copyright © 2009 by Syke Jethani

This title is also available as a Zondervan ebook. Visit www.zondervan.com/ebooks.

This title is also available in a Zondervan audio edition. Visit www.zondervan.fm.

Requests for information should be addressed to:

Zondervan, Grand Rapids, Michigan 49530

Library of Congress Cataloging-in-Publication Data

Jethani, Skye, 1976–
        The divine commodity : discovering a faith beyond consumer Christianity / Skye Jethani.
            p.   cm.
        Includes bibliographical references.
        ISBN 978-0-310-28375-1 (hardcover)
            1. Christianity and culture. 2. Consumption (Economics)—Religious aspects—Christianity. I. Title.
BR115.C8J47   2009
261.0973—dc22   2008036197

Interior design by Mark Sheeres

Printed in the United States of America

---

09 10 11 12 13 14 15 • 24 23 22 21 20 19 18 17 16 15 14 13 12 11 10 9 8 7 6 5 4 3 2 1

For *Life*, *Laughter*, and *Light*.
"Surely the kingdom of heaven belongs to such as these."

CONTENTS

INTRODUCTION

When I have a terrible need of—shall I say the word—religion, then I go out and paint the stars.
Vincent van Gogh

Not long ago I was attending a ministry conference at a very large church. The setting was impressive by any measure. The mammoth auditorium sat thousands in cushioned theater seats rising heavenward. Wherever I looked a dozen flat-panel displays crammed my field of vision with presenters flashing their high-definition smiles. And the stage was alive, a mechanical beast to behold. It was moving fluidly, breathing smoke, and shooting lasers through its digital chameleon skin. The band members were spread across the platform as jagged teeth in the beast's mouth, and the drummer was precariously suspended from the ceiling like a pagan offering. But even this spectacle could not hold me. In fact, with each passing minute I felt a growing need to escape.

I should disclose that sitting through an entire church service has always been difficult for me. As a child I would tell my mother I had to use the bathroom. Then I would slip out of the sanctuary to sit under the crabapple trees. That kind of behavior was excusable for a child, but I still do it, and now I'm a pastor. Sitting through a worship service is a basic requirement for ordination, but sometimes I still slip out—usually to sit under a tree or visit with the children in the nursery. I suppose I'm not setting a good example, but I don't do it too often and I'm always mindful to get back in time to preach the sermon.

The man suffers from Attention Deficit Disorder might be your first assumption. But I don't have ADD, though at least that would be a face-saving explanation for my behavior. It was something else that compelled me out of my theater seat and past the other worshipers attending the ministry conference. I left via the back entrance, walked through the mezzanine, and outside to a lonely balcony.

It was dusk. The moon was low on the horizon and the first stars were appearing. With the beauty of creation unfurled before me, and the glitz of American Christianity behind me, I began to ponder: *Is this what Jesus envisioned? Is this why he came, and suffered, and died? Is this why he*

conquered death and evil, so that we might congregate for multimedia wor-
ship extravaganzas in his name? On that balcony, taking the chilled air into
my body and watching the stars appear, I met with God in silence—my
questions filling the space between us.

Over a century ago another struggling Christian fled the church to
find God in the stars. Vincent van Gogh is remembered for his volatile
mental health, severing his ear, and later taking his life. But the tortured
artist also had a volatile relationship with Christianity, oscillating between
devotion and rejection. At one time his fervor was so intense he became a
missionary. Later he announced, "That God of the clergymen, he is for me
as dead as a doornail,"[1] and called himself "no friend of present-day Christianity."[2] His paintings and letters show us a man wrestling to synthesize
his faith with modern thought. But his struggle was primarily with the
institutional church, not Christ. In his final years, as his mental illness
became more severe, van Gogh reveals a profound devotion to Jesus while
remaining disillusioned with the church. His most celebrated painting
from this period, *Starry Night*, captures this sentiment. *(See color insert,
Image 1.)*

The scene of a quiet hamlet beneath a churning sky of stars was com-
posed from his imagination. For this reason *Starry Night* depicts the vistas
of van Gogh's soul more than the countryside surrounding Saint-Rémy,
France. The deep indigo of the sky was used by Vincent to represent the
infinite presence of God, and the heavenly bodies are yellow—van Gogh's
color for sacred love. The divine light of the stars is repeated in the village
below, every home illuminated with the same yellow warmth. For Vincent,
God's loving presence in the heavens was no less real on the earth.

But there is one building in van Gogh's imaginary village with no light,
no divine presence—the church. Its silent darkness speaks van Gogh's judgment that the institutional church was full of "icy coldness." Like many
people today, van Gogh struggled to find God in the confines of institutional, programmatic religion. Instead, he found himself drawn outside the
respectable piety of the church to commune with peasants and prostitutes.
And his devotion to Christ was inspired by nature—the radiance of sunflowers, the knuckled contortion of olive trees, and the silent providence of
the stars. Rather than visiting the church, van Gogh said, "When I have a
terrible need of—shall I say the word—religion, then I go out and paint the
stars."[3] Were he alive today and attending the same ministry conference, I
might have met him on the church balcony that night.

Like Vincent a century earlier, I fear the contemporary church is losing its ability to inspire. In a world churning with God's wonders, designed to inspire our imaginations and draw our souls heavenward, the programmatic church is dark by comparison. A more recent painting by pop artist Ron English captures the church's condition today. A parody of van Gogh's work, *Starry Night Urban Sprawl* replaces the original French village with the architecture of consumerism—fast food restaurants and Hollywood icons. The church steeple is crowned with McDonald's golden arches and King Kong straddles the roof. *(See color insert, Image 2.)*

Unlike van Gogh's *Starry Night*, in Ron English's composition the church is not dark. Light diffuses through every window and door, but it is not the sacred yellow light of the stars above. Instead, the church repeats the electric white light of the franchised stores and restaurants around it. It reflects the values of the earth, not the values of the heavens. This church is a corporation, its outreach is marketing, its worship is entertainment, and its god is a commodity. It is the church of Consumer Christianity.

Richard Halverson, former chaplain of the United States Senate, is said to have observed that:

> In the beginning the church was a fellowship of men and women centered on the living Christ. Then the church moved to Greece, where it became a philosophy. Then it moved to Rome, where it became an institution. Next, it moved to Europe, where it became a culture. And, finally, it moved to America, where it became an enterprise.[4]

Van Gogh, English, and Halverson capture the question that drove me to that lonely church balcony. Has the contemporary church been so captivated by the images and methods of the consumer culture that it has forfeited its sacred vocation to be a countercultural agent of God's kingdom in the world? And if it has, what are we to do about it?

History has shown syncretism to the culture is a chronic ailment of the church. Solutions have tended to fall into two categories—return or retreat. Some will argue that the church simply needs to return to its first-century roots. There is a bias among Christians that somehow the early church had it right, and everything after the patristic age has been a corruption of what God intended for his people. But the notion of return has two fatal errors. First, it isn't possible. As much as we might like to experience first-century Christianity, time marches forward and not backward. Secondly, the early church's problems were just as significant as ours. In fact, most of the problems addressed by the letters of the apostles in the New Testament were the result of cultural syncretism. Returning to an earlier era of Christianity simply isn't the solution, no matter how romantic it may sound.

The other common answer to a church overly syncretized to the culture has been retreat—abandoning the church to establish another, supposedly more faithful, community. The Qumran sect, authors of the Dead Sea Scrolls, took this approach around the time of Christ. Some monastic orders originated in this manner, and a number of Protestant denominations were born from schisms with other churches in pursuit of ecclesiastical purity. But the retreat solution simply won't work in response to Consumer Christianity. Not only is escape incongruent with the mission the church has been given, it is also impossible. We live, and move, and have our being in a consumer cosmos. The global economy and interconnection of markets and resources means every time we eat a meal, listen to music, put on clothing, or read a book (like this one), we are being consumers.

But there is a difference between living in a consumer society and adopting a consumer worldview. Our faithful Christian predecessors lived within the Roman Empire, but their minds and hearts were not beholden to Caesar. Their citizenship was not to Rome. Likewise, we must learn to exist in a consumer empire but not forfeit our souls at its altar. This means addressing the issue at a level beyond mere behaviors.

Christian critiques of consumerism usually focus on the danger of idolatry—the temptation to make material goods the center of life rather than God. However legitimate and commonplace the evil of materialism may be, it misses the real threat consumerism poses. Consuming goods (a behavior) is not inherently wrong; as contingent beings our Creator has designed us to consume resources to survive. Rather than a behavior, this book will approach consumerism as a set of presuppositions most of us have been formed to carry without question or critique. More than merely an economic system, it is the framework through which we understand everything including the gospel, the church, and God himself. Consumerism is the dominant worldview of North Americans. As such, it is competing with the kingdom of heaven for the hearts and imaginations of God's people.

I hope to tackle the problematic union of consumerism and Christianity in three ways. First, each chapter will show how our formation as consumers has distorted an element of our faith. For example, how we've turned God into a consumable product, or the breakdown of community through market-driven individualism. The pervasive influence of consumerism must be revealed and critiqued before we can hope to move any further.

Secondly, the book seeks to energize an alternative vision of faith. The values of consumerism have captured the imaginations of both the religious and irreligious in our day. Our minds are so captivated by these ideas that we've lost the ability to think an alternative thought. As a result, the imagination has become the critical battleground between the kingdom of God and consumerism, and before we can hope to live differently we must have our minds released from consumerism's grip and captivated again by Christ. As Thomas Kelly contends, before we can live in full obedience to God we must be given a flaming vision of such an existence. This burning image comes to us through our intuitive faculties. "Holy is imagination, the gateway of Reality into our hearts."[5]

To accomplish this, I have approached the structure of each chapter the way we encounter a van Gogh painting. Like other post-Impressionist artists, van Gogh used brilliant and contrasting colors applied with short, staccato brushstrokes. At close range the subjects of his paintings were indecipherable, a formless abstract of color and texture. One must step away from the canvas for the colors to fuse and the eye to discern the subject. Likewise, the chapters that follow are impressionist in form. They are comprised of short, seemingly incongruent scenes of personal narrative, biblical exposition, and cultural observation. But with distance and reflection they fuse in the mind's eye to construct a discernable theme. My intent is for the reader's imagination, and not merely his or her intellect, to be awakened and nourished with an alternative vision of faith from the one we've inherited from our consumer formation.

Toward this end, I recommend reading the book in community. I have found the discipline of godly conversation to be indispensable to my growth, and processing the concepts in each chapter with others may ignite your imagination into a fire that the single spark of your mind could never muster alone. Similarly, the content of the book is drawn from my experience and setting, not yours. While I hope there is considerable congruency, each reader must still wrestle with the implications of each chapter for his or her own life. If reading a self-help book is like being served a meal, this book is like being invited into the kitchen. Here you are encouraged to pull from the cupboards and apply the concepts yourself. This creative work is best done in community with friends.

Of course, I do not want my readers to have to fend for themselves entirely. So, the third way this book will try to address the challenge of consumerism is by prescribing actions of re-formation. With our imaginations freed from the confinements of consumerism we still require the means to implement our faith—methods of manifesting in the world what our illuminated minds have envisioned. Within each chapter I will explore a spiritual practice that can aid us, individually and communally, in living a post-consumer Christianity.

Consumer Christianity, while promising to strengthen our souls with an entertaining faith, has left us malnourished with an anemic view of God, faith, church, and mission. Van Gogh sought Christ by painting the stars, a divine distraction from the institutional religion of his day. I have found my divine distractions to be sitting under a crabapple tree, playing with a child, or standing under a starry sky on a lonely balcony. (In the epilogue you will hear how my evening on the church balcony ended and the unexpected lesson I learned.) I hope this book will be a divine distraction for you, one that rekindles your dormant imagination and helps us all reimagine what our faith can be.

CHAPTER 1

SLUMBER OF THE IMAGINATION

Do not quench your inspiration and your imagination;
do not become the slave of your model.
Vincent van Gogh

WALTOPIA

Soaring above the wetlands of central Florida, like an iridescent pearl on green velvet, is Spaceship Earth. The massive geodesic sphere is the heart of Disney's Epcot Center, and an architectural monument to Walt Disney's greatest dream. The sublime beauty of the silver orb is matched only by its colossal failure.

The final years of Walt Disney's visionary life were consumed with the goal of solving the problems facing the world's cities by utilizing advances in science, industry, and urban design. After building Disneyland in California, Walt purchased forty-seven square miles of Florida wilderness not simply to reproduce his West Coast theme park, but to build a fully functional city of the future. He called it E.P.C.O.T. — Experimental Prototype Community of Tomorrow.

In his final film, Walt Disney revealed his plans for Epcot that included schools, residential neighborhoods, parks, churches, advanced public transportation, even skyscrapers and a sports arena. He said Epcot would be a showcase that will "always be in a state of becoming. It will never cease to be a living blueprint of the future where people actually live a life they can't find anyplace else in the world."[1]

In Walt Disney's imagination every detail of Epcot was already real. He even envisioned how the garbage would be collected. But others believed Walt's vision was so fantastical, so beyond convention, that it couldn't possibly be realized. Behind his back company managers referred to his dream as "Waltopia" — from the Greek word *utopia* meaning "no place."

After Disney's unexpected death in 1966, his successors didn't know how to proceed with Epcot. Rather than an advanced city unlike any in the world, company executives who lacked Walt's ability to see beyond proven formulas retreated to a more conventional concept. The new president of the Disney Company said Epcot was now being reconsidered "from the point of view of economics, operations, technology, and market potential."[2]

By the time Epcot opened on October 1, 1982, little remained of Walt's dream. Rather than a stream of residents commuting to their first day at work, it was an ocean of tourists who walked beneath the reflective belly of Spaceship Earth ready to buy souvenirs and consume prefabricated experiences. The grand city of tomorrow never lived beyond Walt's imagination. Instead, Epcot became a theme park — a pragmatic and proven idea Disney's managers could execute and stockholders could embrace.

Today, Epcot is the least popular amusement park in Disney's vacation kingdom. Incapable of inspiring the citizens of the world as Walt had dreamed, it has become a subject of ridicule and mockery. Comedian P. J. O'Rourke has remarked, "With Epcot Center the Disney Corporation has accomplished something I didn't think possible in today's world. They have created a land of make-believe that's worse than regular life."[3]

The gleaming pearl on the horizon of central Florida's wilderness is a reminder that imagination is in a battle with conventionality, and conventionality is a powerful foe.

TRIUMPH AND TRAGEDY

In July 2003, not far from the shadow of Epcot's silver sphere in Orlando, ten thousand Christian retailers gathered for the fifty-fourth annual Christian Booksellers Association convention. The CBA represents the $4.2 billion industry that sells Bibles, books, bubblegum, and bracelets to Christian consumers. The economic power wielded by the CBA has grown so rapidly that President George W. Bush has even taken notice.

Bush, whose ascent to the presidency would not have been possible without conservative evangelicals, addressed the 2003 CBA convention via video. "You know as I do the power of faith can transform lives," he said. "You bring the Good News to a world hungry for hope and comfort and encouragement."[4] Interestingly, Bush was praising Christian retailers, not churches, for spreading the light of Christ. The fact that the president of the United States, the most powerful political figure on the planet, would address the merchants of Christian books and baubles reveals the economic and political influence Christian consumers have attained.

The other memorable appearance at the 2003 CBA convention was actor/director Mel Gibson. The Hollywood hero and devout Roman Catholic gave a preview of his upcoming film *The Passion of the Christ*. Gibson's movie was promoted as a way for Christian retailers to leverage the Easter holiday. The CBA's president said, "We want to play a role in reclaiming the holiday for Christ. We want to draw people into our stores and drive seekers into the church."[5] Of course, *The Passion of the Christ* became one of the most profitable films in history, grossing nearly $700 million worldwide and triggering a new wave of Christian-friendly Hollywood productions.

The presence of both political and pop-culture royalty at the CBA convention would have been unimaginable just a few years earlier. In the mid-twentieth century some feared America would follow the path of Europe, where the church atrophied to become an emaciated shell of its former glory. That fear drove evangelical Christians to seek cultural, political, and economic influence as a way of ensuring survival. The 2003 CBA convention represented the culmination of their cultural revolution. Like Epcot's beautiful geodesic sphere, the church had soared to become a powerful icon on the horizon of the American cultural landscape. But like Epcot, the church's stunning ascent has been matched only by its colossal failure.

Christian researcher George Barna concludes, "American Christianity has largely failed since the middle of the twentieth century because Jesus' modern-day disciples do not act like Jesus."[6] During the same half century that evangelicals were climbing to the pinnacle of cultural influence, the church has largely lost its ability to transform lives and teach people to practice the values championed by Christ. Research conducted by sociologists and pollsters shows that "evangelical Christians are as likely to embrace lifestyles every bit as hedonistic, materialistic, self-centered, and sexually immoral as the world in general."[7] Despite the influence of Jesus Christ over Washington, Hollywood, and Wall Street, his power over the hearts and minds of people in America is far less evident.

Along with suffering a deficit of qualitative distinctiveness, the church is also losing ground quantitatively. The percentage of Americans engaged in a local congregation has been declining for years. In 1990 approximately

20 percent of the population attended church on any given weekend. By 2004 the figure had dropped to 17 percent. If the trend continues, by 2050 only 11 percent of Americans will attend church. Although megachurches have multiplied across the fruited plains, the numbers show that Christianity in America has been consolidating and not expanding.[8]

Parallel Universe

The challenge facing Christianity today is not a lack of motivation or resources, but a failure of imagination.

Walt Disney's successors wanted to honor their founder's dream. That laudable motivation is what kept the Epcot project alive. The problem was not their motivation; it was their lack of imagination. They did not possess Disney's ability to see beyond what was conventionally possible. They simply could not see the city he wanted to build in their mind's eye. As a result they reinterpreted Epcot through the only framework they could comprehend — pragmatics, economics, and market potential.

Likewise, the paradoxical rise of Christian political/economic influence and decline of Christian moral influence is not the product of devious or ignoble motivation. Christian leaders in America are largely admirable men and women who passionately love God and genuinely desire to honor Christ. Many sacrifice time, income, and emotional energy giving themselves to what they believe matters most: Christ and his kingdom. And we certainly do not lack resources. In fact, based on the CBA's own numbers we have spent more money equipping the church than any other Christians in history.

Our deficiency is not motivation or money, but imagination. Our ability to live Christianly and be the church corporately has failed because we do not believe it is possible. Like Disney's successors we simply cannot imagine how to carry out the fantastical mission of our leader. Wanting to obey Christ but lacking his imagination, we reinterpret the mission of the church through the only framework comprehendible to us — the one we've inherited from our consumer culture.

Many books about the crisis facing the American church have been added to our shelves in recent years. Most of these well-intentioned reads suggest a new model of church, a new method of cultural engagement, or a new strategy for missions. Certainly there is a place for models, strategies, and methods, but before a solution can be implemented it must be imagined. Without imagination any solution we conceive will be rooted to the very system we must transcend. How can a prisoner plot his escape if he doesn't believe a world exists outside the prison walls? The prisoner's imagination must be free before his body can follow. As Albert Einstein observed, "Problems cannot be solved with the same consciousness that created them." And Walter Brueggemann declares, "Questions of implementation are of no consequence until the vision can be imagined. The imagination must come before implementation. Our culture is competent to implement almost anything and to imagine almost nothing."[9]

The emergence of a Christian subculture that parallels the secular culture in every way reveals the captivity of our imaginations. With a speed matched only by the Chinese black market, Christian merchandisers produce knockoffs of every secular phenomenon virtually overnight. Whether a new music genre, diet program, or fashion trend, you are sure to find a Jesus version in your local Christian store in time for Christmas. (I was recently given a poker chip that said, "Jesus went all in for you. So ante up and give your heart to him.") If imitation is the highest form of flattery, than Christians have become pop culture's most devoted admirers.

This bizarre parallel universe is not limited to kitschy Christian knick-knacks. We also manage our churches with repackaged secular business principles and methodologies pioneered by marketers. A prominent pastor was asked what was distinctly spiritual about his leadership. The pastor responded, "There's nothing distinctly spiritual.... One of the criticisms I get is 'Your church is so corporate....' And I say, 'OK, you're right. Now why is that a bad model?' " Justifying his use of secular business models the pastor said, "A principle is a principle, and God created all the principles."[10]

In his defense, for decades ministers have been conditioned by books, conferences, and seminaries to revere how secular corporations accomplish their work. It is assumed that the way Home Depot or Starbucks reacts to consumers' desires is how the church ought to react as well. Whether one is selling Chryslers, Coca-Cola, or Christ is irrelevant, the principles of marketing and persuasion apply equally to all. So, why not learn from the biggest and best? Lyle Schaller, one of the most popular church consultants, has said, "The big issue ... is not whether one applauds or disapproves of the growth of consumerism. The central issue is that consumerism is now a fact of life."[11] In his book, *The Very Large Church*, Schaller goes on to coach pastors on how to appeal to spiritual consumers, but he never expects the church to transcend or transform these cultural values. This posture of resignation to consumer culture reveals the utter captivity of our imaginations.

The eagerness to defend conventionality found in both church leaders and lay people explains why sociologists can no longer differentiate the lives of Christians from non-Christians, or the behavior of churches from corporations. We have lost the ability to imagine. We have abandoned the vision that Christianity is an alternative way. We cannot see our lives, our households, or our churches operating any differently than the world around us. As Brueggemann says, "The key pathology of our time, which seduces us all, is the reduction of our imagination so that we are too numbed, satiated, and co-opted to do serious imaginative work."[12] Our spiritual imaginations have fallen asleep on the comfortable mattress of the consumer culture, and before any remedy for the church can be prescribed our dormant imaginations must be stirred from their slumber.

A CHILD WILL LEAD THEM

"Come on. That's a good girl. Come on." I peeked over the screen of my laptop. Alone in the family room with Zoe, my four-year-old daughter, I wondered who she was talking to. I had been checking my email while she entertained herself with the dolls and paper and crayons strewn on the floor. "Come on, you're almost there," she said.

"Who are you talking to, Zoe?" I asked. She was walking slowly through the room holding one hand behind her.

"Sandy," she replied. I scanned the dolls on the floor. There was Baby Blue, Baby Pink, Baby Red, and the most beloved Baby Too (a name Zoe assumed for the doll because her mother and I would frequently ask, "Would you like your baby too?"). But I saw no doll that might be a new Baby Sandy.

"Who is Sandy?" I asked.

"Daddy!" she sighed and rolled her eyes with the condescension of a teenager. "Sandy is my horse." The *duh* at the end of her sentence was implied as she motioned to the invisible filly in the middle of our family room. "I'm taking her to the barn so she can eat her lunch."

"And what are you going to feed her?" I was happy to play along.

Zoe shook her head. "Horses eat hay, Dad." A fact so well known that my question was clearly out of line even in Zoe's imaginary world. She proceeded to the kitchen/barn where Sandy enjoyed her lunch.

My brief encounter with Zoe's imagination resurrected memories of my own. A photo album opened in my mind, and I saw faded scenes from a friendship long ago. Wanda and I playing on the swing set. The two of us gazing at the fish bowl. And, of course, Wanda and I discovering the endless joy of Legos. She was my imaginary friend. "Wanda from Toronto" is what I called her when I was four years old. (To my knowledge I've never been to Toronto, and to this day Wanda remains my only friend from the city.) Her unannounced appearance at a family gathering or dinner party was always a point of conflict. My older brother and cousins loved to tease me, but I learned how to defend my unconventional relationship with Wanda. That's what friends do.

With Sandy eating her lunch in the kitchen/barn and Zoe brushing her mane, I reflected on the distant joy of a childish imagination. *What happened to Wanda?* I thought. She returned to Toronto many years ago and never visited me again. She probably sensed that she was no longer welcomed. Like the disciples who tried to keep the children away from Jesus, most of my adult life has been spent repressing my imagination. *Such things are childish and have no place in the serious Christian life*, I thought. The fertile land of imagination is a terrain we pass through, not a field we cultivate. Didn't the apostle Paul say, "When I was a child, I talked like a child, I thought like a child, I reasoned like a child. When I became a man, I put childish ways behind me."[13]

I have been told many reasons for keeping the imagination out of my Christian life. *The imagination is for New Age spirituality. Imagination is sinful. Imagination leads to heresy. You don't need imagination, you have the Bible.* But then I remember Jesus calling the children. "Let the little children come to me and do not hinder them,"[14] he said. I so easily forget that Jesus welcomes all of me, even my childishness. I wonder what that boy felt when Jesus put him in front of those men bickering about who was the greatest. I wonder how he felt as Jesus placed his hand on his shoulders and said to them, "Truly, I say to you, unless you turn and become like children, you will never enter the kingdom of heaven."[15]

Jesus' adult followers suffered from a chronic lack of imagination. Their minds were shackled by conventionality. When a storm threatened their safety on the sea they panicked. After calming the wind and waves with just a word, Jesus rebuked their lack of faith. Shortly after seeing Jesus feed four thousand people with just a few loaves and fish, the disciples started whining about not having any food for their journey. "Do you not yet perceive or understand?" Jesus chided. "Having eyes do you not see, and having ears do you not hear?"[16] And when they bickered about who would be greatest in God's kingdom, Jesus put a little boy before them and said, "Whoever humbles himself like this child is the greatest."[17]

Consider the servant girl Rhoda. The Christians in Jerusalem gathered in Mary's home to pray fervently for Peter's release from Herod's jail. During the night as the believers prayed, an angel appeared and sprung Peter from his cell just hours before his scheduled execution. But even while following the angel through the streets, Peter believed the entire event was a dream. When he reached Mary's house and knocked on the door, Rhoda joyfully announced to the adults, still in their prayer meeting perhaps, that Peter had arrived. (Rhoda herself was so surprised that she forgot to let him in.) The adults replied, "You are out of your mind!" Despite Rhoda's insistence that it was Peter, they refused to believe her. In this humorous account not a single adult could imagine God actually intervening and rescuing Peter, not even Peter himself! Obedience led them to pray for Peter's rescue, but their imaginations could not follow. Only Rhoda, a young girl, had the capacity to believe the unbelievable.

A child is precious in God's kingdom because her imagination has not yet fallen asleep. The culture's conventionality has not yet hijacked her ability to believe. To a child the world is still full of mystery and possibility. A word can calm a storm; a few fish and loaves can feed thousands; a touch can heal the blind. A child can readily imagine the alternative reality of God's kingdom that adults struggle to see.

A RAY FROM ON HIGH

In the 1800s art and technology clashed. For centuries Western art had been on a journey toward realism. Through the Middle Ages, the Renaissance, and the Enlightenment, artistic techniques had steadily progressed. The flat two-dimensional illustrations common before the Renaissance gave way to realistic scenes that showed an understanding of perspective, shape, light, and color theory. By the mid-nineteenth century the most celebrated artists were Realists who produced paintings in a style referred to as *trompe d'œil*—literally able to "trick the eye."

But in the late nineteenth century a new technology was attracting a lot of attention in Europe and America—photography. With a device now able to produce realistic images in seconds, the reliance on painters to present reality was undermined. Slowly the artistic school of Realism declined and a new one emerged. A group of artists known as Impressionists leveraged the one significant advantage paint still held over photography—color. Artists like Monet and Seurat used advances in light and atmospheric theory to paint with dots or small strokes of color. (Their works were the forerunners of the pixilated displays that dominate our digital society.) But Impressionism did not shake the central tenant of Realism; it still sought to present the world as seen by the human eye.

Then came Vincent. Van Gogh had little respect for photography. He considered it a lifeless and abhorrent art form. He said the same of painting that sought to precisely mimic what the eye saw. Instead, he admired the more interpretive paintings of Millet and Lhermitte. In their works, he said, "All reality is also at the same time symbolic. They are different from what are called realists."[18] Vincent believed art should do more than present reality; it should *re*present reality by uncovering the truth that is not apparent to the naked eye. But unlike his friend Gauguin, van Gogh was not in favor of total abstraction either. He preferred the tension between realism and abstraction, what some have termed Expressionism.

Commenting on this middle way, he says, "I exaggerate, sometimes I make changes in a motif; but for all that, I do not invent the whole picture; on the contrary, I find it already in nature, only it must be disentangled."[19] His paintings were not flights of fancy without any basis in reality; neither were they literal reproductions of nature. Unlike abstract paintings, van Gogh's works have discernable subjects: a tree, a farmer, a vase of sunflowers, a church. But van Gogh did not present these subjects as they actually appear to the eye. Instead he painted them as he experienced them; he sought to "disentangled" the essence of his subject from the literal scene. As a result, Vincent's paintings were the synthesis of what his eye saw and what his imagination perceived. He made the invisible visible. Usually this was accomplished with the symbolic and emotional use of color. While painting in the countryside of Arles, he wrote:

> I am always in hope of making a discovery there, to express the love of two lovers by a wedding of two complementary colors, their mingling and their opposition, the mysterious vibrations of kindred tones. To express the thought of a brow by the radiance of a light tone against a somber background. To express hope by some distant star, the eagerness of a soul by a sunset radiance. Certainly there is no fake realism (*trompe d'œil*) in that, but isn't it something that actually exists?[20]

Vincent wanted to express ideas in his paintings such as hope, love, and grief. He sought to make these invisible realities visible through color. He understood the way colors could trigger different emotions, how each one carried its own personality. Vincent saw red as passionate and dangerous. Blue he associated with the mysterious and the infinite. But the color Vincent preferred most of all was yellow. As the brightest hue on the color wheel, it arrests the eye. Van Gogh recognized something divine about yellow's loud magnetism. As the eye is drawn to the vivid warmth of golden light, so the heart is drawn to the radiant warmth of God's love. He used the color to represent sacred love in many of his compositions, and to Vincent yellow symbolized the presence of the *rayon d'en haut*—French for "the ray of light from above."

In many of his canvases yellow light pours down from the heavens like golden rain. The light itself appears to be a tangible object, a physical presence in the scene that illuminates the faces it touches. Given van Gogh's association of yellow with God, we shouldn't be surprised that many of the biblical scenes he painted are dominated by the color. For example, in *The Raising of Lazarus*, Jesus is noticeably absent. *(See color insert, Image 3.)* Instead, Vincent flooded the entire composition with yellow light, a ray from on high, implying Christ's presence and divine power. But it is van Gogh's use of yellow in nonreligious paintings that is most intriguing. Whether a sky saturated with sunlight, gold harvest fields, or yellow stars swirling in the heavens, Vincent saw God's invisible love in virtually everything he painted.

During his lifetime some mocked Vincent's work as childish. Those beholden to Realism didn't understand his desire to paint the unseen realities of the world. Like the crowds who dismissed Jesus' words, they had eyes but they could not see. Vincent believed the ability to perceive the unseen was achieved only by the grace of God. He wrote, "You need a certain dose of inspiration, a ray from on high, that is not in ourselves, in order to do beautiful things."[21] He believed there was more to the world than what science could detect, more than what the camera could capture. In this way van Gogh was a painter-prophet. He revealed visions and interpreted hidden truths. He didn't merely present the world as it is; he *re*presented it as one full of God's presence and love. But to see this world a person needs more than eyes. He or she needs a ray from on high, an imagination awakened and illuminated by God.

DISENTANGLING REALITY

Van Gogh did not abandon reality, but he was not shackled by it either. He saw the world through an illuminated imagination, with a light that he believed came from God. Without this light we are confined to a *trompe d'œil* existence, one in which we see only a facsimile of the world in two dimensions. What most people call "real" is only a piece of reality because the real-real remains hidden to them. What's missing is the ray from on high to awaken the imagination and enable us to perceive more than the eye sees. This ray is the grace of God that, as van Gogh says, empowers us to disentangle reality.

Learning to see the world as it truly is—saturated with the presence and love of God—should be the essence of Christian discipleship, or what many call spiritual formation. Unfortunately, most ministries and churches have focused their efforts at spiritual formation upon two areas—knowledge and skills—and have neglected the vital role of the imagination. This amounts to teaching deaf students how to read sheet music. Until their ability to hear sound is restored, their capacity and motivation to produce music will be severely limited.

The neglect of the imagination is not a recent development. Since the Enlightenment's coronation of knowledge, the church has poured enormous energy into communicating facts about God through sermons, classes, Sunday school, and small groups. It was relatively recently that an increasing number of voices began challenging the effectiveness of information-based formation. Generations of Christians had brains full of biblical knowledge and doctrine, but their lives showed little evidence of the transformation Jesus called forth in his Sermon on the Mount.

In response, during the late twentieth century, many churches and ministries began to shift their focus from dispensing knowledge to teaching skills. This model focuses on training people how to ____ (fill in the blank). Preaching moved away from expositing entire books of the Bible and unpacking doctrines to presenting the pragmatics of living a Christian life. These sermons are easy to identify by their numeric qualifiers: 5 Principles of Parenting; 7 Habits of a Happy Marriage; 3 Biblical Blessings for Businessmen. Outside the church an astounding number of conferences, seminars, workshops, and curricula have been developed with the "how to" perspective.

While necessary components of spiritual formation, both knowledge and skills miss the imaginative aspect of the human spirit that Jesus frequently targeted. Without an imagination illuminated by God and caught up in the alternative reality of his kingdom, skills and knowledge are severely limited in their ability to transform because we can still only see a two-dimensional *trompe d'œil* world. We remain trapped in whatever delusive reality our culture presents to us. Oswald Chambers understood this danger. He knew that if "your imagination of God is starved then when you come up against difficulties, you have no power, you can only endure in darkness."[22] The critical role of the imagination is affirmed by how Jesus constructed his own ministry.

The Gospel writers show Jesus very infrequently teaching skills, and only periodically conveying didactic knowledge. Instead the Gospels are dominated by Jesus telling stories and weaving parables. He used these verbal Trojan horses to sneak radical truths past his listeners' defenses and into the chamber where their imaginations slumbered. And as they began to awaken, Jesus' stories illuminated a new vision of the world. They disentangled reality for his listeners, and his disciples slowly perceived the kingdom of God that Jesus saw all around him. It was a kingdom that defied the conventionality of his day. A kingdom where rebellious criminals are embraced by God like a loving father; where the poor and the weak are welcomed to God's table; where the servant is honored and the powerful are brought low. It was a radical vision not everyone could accept. Some were too enslaved by the cultural conventions, too entangled in realism for their imaginations to be awakened. These people heard Jesus tell stories about trees, fields, treasures, or seeds—but nothing more. They could hear, but not understand. They could see, but could not perceive.[23]

But those whose imaginations were set free, those illuminated by the ray from on high, saw with new eyes. They understood the radical vision of Jesus and went on to transform the world. The book of Acts shows them overcoming kings and subverting empires, raising the dead and healing the blind, living in unity and loving the unlovable. But they did not achieve these things through the wisdom or methods of the world, but through the foolishness of God. And like Jesus, their ability to see the unseen and speak of a more *real* real made them incredibly dangerous people. They were a threat to the fake reality, the *trompe d'œil* deception, established by the powers and authorities of the world.

Stephen was a man whose imagination had been awakened by Christ. He was no longer enslaved by the conventionality of first-century Judea, and he saw a world illuminated by the light of God's kingdom. So he was marked as a dangerous man, someone who would not conform to accepted practices and ideals. Surrounded by those still imprisoned by conventionality and entangled in delusive realism, Stephen, full of the Holy Spirit, announced the real reality he saw: "Behold, I see the heavens opened, and the Son of Man standing at the right hand of God."[24] The others, in vigorous defense of a two-dimensional world, cried out and covered their ears. Then they rushed at Stephen and killed him.

If we are to effectively make disciples of Jesus Christ and teach them to obey everything he commanded, we cannot neglect the imagination. Knowledge and skills are important, but neither will be employable if the mind is still imprisoned by the conventionality of the surrounding culture. Like Jesus, we must find ways of getting past defensive walls and enter the chamber where peoples' imaginations are sleeping and stir them from hibernation. The alternative is the creation of nominal Christians—people possessing knowledge about God but lacking the eyes to see him in the world or practice the alternative values of his kingdom.

Vincent van Gogh warned other artists, "Do not quench your inspiration and your imagination; do not become the slave of your model."[25] By constructing a Christian subculture that mimics the consumer culture, we have become slaves to our model. We have diminished our ability to imagine the fuller reality presented by Christ. But awakening our imaginations is not something we can accomplish unilaterally. We need the ray from on high that is not from ourselves. We need a childlike faith that surrenders wholly to the grace of God and awaits his illuminating touch. Without this humility our attempts to follow after Christ and advance his mission, although pure in motivation, will be fruitless.

CRYPTO-CHRISTIANS

In 1549 the Jesuit missionary Francis Xavier introduced Christianity to Japan. As the church grew rapidly to 300,000 believers, the shoguns became uneasy with the European influence over their country. In 1641, the missionaries were expelled from Japan, and Christians were required to register as Buddhists or Shintoists. Those who refused were pursued and executed. The brutal persecution cleansed Japan from virtually all Western influence.

The shoguns, however, were unaware that some continued to hold to their Christian faith. Known as Crypto-Christians, or Kakure, their external lives were indistinguishable from other Japanese. They adopted the practices, form, and appearance of non-Christians to ensure survival. The Crypto-Christians even constructed Buddhist shrines in their homes with secret compartments where Christian icons and statues were hidden and where prayers were offered to the "closet god."

The strategy of adopting Japanese cultural forms to mask their Christian faith continued for 240 years, but if their intention was to preserve the faith they had been taught by the missionaries, the plan backfired. Over time the Crypto-Christians confused their Christian beliefs and their Japanese disguises. The result was the emergence of a hybrid religion no longer adhering to the doctrines of orthodox Christianity. When Europeans regained entrance to Japan in the nineteenth century, they were astonished to see communities of hidden Christians living in the hills around Nagasaki. This amazement waned, however, when they discovered the faith of these forgotten Christians was hardly Christianity. "Although the faith followed by the underground Christians had the outward appearances of Christianity, the vital content and spirit of the religion evolved into something entirely different.... It would be more accurate to call it a folk religion altogether Japanese in spirit and content."[26]

Thousands of Kakure still exist in Japan today, and at least eighty house churches continue to worship the "closet god" by reciting rituals in an indecipherable amalgam of Japanese and Latin. When Pope John Paul II visited Japan in 1981, he met with the leaders of the Kakure community to welcome them back into the fold of the Catholic Church. "We have no interest in joining his church," one Crypto-Christian said. "We, and nobody else, are true Christians."[27]

Ironically, it is often our zeal to protect our faith that leads to its loss. Abram was called to leave his country and follow the alternative ways of Yahweh. But when feeling threatened, Abram disguised himself by adopting Egyptian practices, allowing his wife to be taken into Pharaoh's house. Later, God called Israel to be separate from the other nations — to be an alternative people, a holy nation, a royal priesthood. But in time they felt threatened and asked God for a king to protect them. The peoples' desire was innocent enough. They still wanted to follow God; they just wanted to do it in a way more "like the nations around them." The Lord warned that a king would rule over them just as Pharaoh had in Egypt, but the people refused to listen.

The record of the Old Testament affirms what the Lord predicted. Even the kings who desired to follow the ways of the Lord found it difficult not to act like the pagan nations. In time prophets denounced God's people for becoming indistinguishable from their neighbors — not caring for aliens, orphans, and widows; failing to act justly; cheating their countrymen; amassing gold and silver; exploiting the poor; and all the while hypocritically honoring God with their festivals and songs. They had become Crypto-Hebrews. Ultimately, Israel's imagination became so captivated by the nations and their idols that God allowed their bodies to be captivated as well. First the Assyrians and later the Babylonians destroyed the remaining symbols of Israel's commitment to God and took the people into exile.

In our cultural quest for survival, driven by our fear of irrelevance, have evangelicals become Crypto-Christians? Have we clothed our faith with the forms of our American culture to the point that our Christianity has morphed into something entirely different—a folk religion altogether consumerist in spirit and content? Like the Kakure of Japan, are we holding so tightly to our faith that we cannot sense it has already slipped between our fingers? By yielding its imagination to the forms around it, has the church, like ancient Israel, lost the ability to be an alternative people of God? Is Walter Brueggemann correct: "The contemporary American church is so largely enculturated to the American ethos of consumerism that is has little power to believe or to act"?[28]

WELCOME BACK, WANDA

From Abraham to Israel, the apostles to the Kakure, since the beginning the imagination of God's people has been under attack from cultural conventionality. And the evidence suggests that the contemporary church, seeking survival and relevancy, has surrendered its alternative imagination as well. Rather than pursuing our calling to present a vision of a world filled with God's power and love, the contemporary church merely presents the world as people already know it. It is a two-dimensional facsimile of the consumer culture, albeit with a Jesus fish imprint. The result is an impotent church at home in our world, a church that poses no threat to the powers of conventionality and with no prophetic voice to awaken the imagination.

Like my friend Wanda from Toronto, the Christian imagination left the church many years ago and took with it the childlike joy of faith—the joy of believing in a God without limits. But there is a way to get it back. This way is not discovered by church business consultants, marketing gurus, or how-to experts. It is not found by people who only see the world as it appears, but by people who see the world as it truly is—a cosmos filled with the light of God revealed to those who have eyes to see. This way is illuminated by children, those whose imaginations have not yet fallen asleep. This way is illuminated by Rhoda, a little girl who believed in God's power when no adult could. This way is illuminated by van Gogh, an artist who ventured to capture more than what was seen. This way is illuminated by Stephen, a disciple whose vision of reality was so threatening he became a martyr. Inspired by their example, in the chapters that follow we will explore how our views of God, worship, community, formation, and mission have been captivated by consumer conventionality and dare to discover an alternative way.

CHAPTER 2

THE CANVAS OF SILENCE

When all sounds cease, God's voice
is heard under the stars.

Vincent van Gogh

INSIGNIFICANT FEELINGS

As I stared up in the darkness the stars seemed layered upon each other, more than I had ever seen before. Had I lived centuries earlier I would have believed that a giant with his feet straddling the horizon had taken a wide brush and painted the arc of stars across the sky. Carl Sagan's voice echoed in my mind, "Billions and billions." I lost myself in the immensity of the heavens; they seemed to envelop me. To remind myself that I was still on the earth I would occasionally move the sand between my toes. *Is that how the stars seem to God—like cosmic grains of sand that pass through his fingers?* I was aware of the presence of my three companions but only peripherally. A hand would break into my field of vision pointing to a shooting star or planet, but that was the extent of our communication—at least with each other.

I was seventeen years old and had seen many night skies before, but none like this. For most of my life the glow of parking lots and shopping malls had diminished the wonders of the heavens, the light of only a few stars able to break through the haze. But standing near the ocean a healthy distance from civilization made this night different. I felt like I was looking at the stars for the first time in my life. And then it occurred to me—I was. I had never seen these stars before. I was standing on a beach in Australia. The southern hemisphere sees an entirely different night sky with different stars and different constellations. This was a side of the universe my eyes had never looked upon before.

An old "Peanuts" cartoon shows Charlie Brown and Sally outside at night gazing at the stars. "Let's go inside and watch television," Charlie Brown says. "I'm beginning to feel insignificant." Like Charlie Brown, any pretense of self-importance I carried melted away as I contemplated the vastness of the universe above me. But there was no television to rescue me this night. My companions on the beach, three other American teenagers—fond of meaningless chatter, crude jokes, and adolescent pontification—joined me in reverent silence. We didn't share the ideas filling our minds as the meteors burned through the atmosphere and the galaxy flickered around us. The scene was too sacred for words. Anything spoken could not possibly add to the experience and would only risk diminishing it.

I have existed for a mere seventeen years, I thought, *but these stars, these silent sentinels, have watched over the earth for ages upon ages.* Strangely, in this moment of reflection I began to feel a deeper bond with my three friends, and indeed all who've watched the heavens. I imagined other people all over the planet gazing up at these same stars this night, and the generations who looked at these stars before me, the first European sailors in the southern seas, and the aborigines who lived here for millennia before them, all of us looking up at the same sky and experiencing the same utterly human emotion—wonder. Does a monkey sit in his tree, pondering the Milky Way, and think, *Wow?* Isn't that what separates us from the animals, our ability to experience awe? We've all lived under this same canopy, and we've all sensed our utter insignificance when confronted by its immensity, and we've all been silenced by its beauty—the mighty and the humble, the educated and the ignorant, the saints and the atheists.

The Liturgy of Saint James is considered the oldest surviving Christian order of worship, dated by some as early as 60 AD. It is the basis for one of my favorite hymns:

> *Let all mortal flesh keep silence,*
> *and with fear and trembling stand;*
> *ponder nothing earthly minded,*
> *for with blessing in his hand*
> *Christ our God to earth descendeth,*
> *our full homage to demand.*

When our imaginations are jolted into contemplating our true insignificance, either by a star-filled sky or some other encounter with the transcendent, our response is always the same—silence. It is the humility any rational creature should exhibit when confronted by a power so immeasurable it defies comprehension. Silence is the beginning of all worship.

After standing on the dark Australian beach for hours, our bodies began to tire and our craned necks started to ache. Our spirits were willing but our flesh was weak. Reluctantly, we left the sacred ground and started to trek back to town and our beds. Eventually words were shared, slowly at first, and with more frequency as the walk continued. We were like astronauts attempting reentry. It was a delicate procedure that could not be done recklessly. From what my friends revealed it became obvious that we had all experienced something similar, something we all struggled to articulate with words, and after that walk home we never tried to again.

OUR WORDY WORLD

Silence is a rare commodity in our world. Everywhere we turn our senses are bombarded with messages both visual and auditory. Henri Nouwen recalls driving through Los Angeles and having the bizarre sense that he was traveling through a giant dictionary. "Wherever I looked there were words trying to take my eyes from the road. They said, 'Use me, take me, buy me, drink me, smell me, touch me, kiss me, sleep with me.' In such a world, who can maintain respect for words?"[1]

Nouwen's problem with our "wordy world," as he calls it, is that the spiritual life must find its origin in silence. Centuries of Christian tradition and practice have verified this fact, and it crosses all denominational and theological camps. The holiness movement required silence to examine the condition of one's soul before God. The Jesuits prescribed silence to engage cycles of desolation and consolation. The Desert Fathers believed solitude and silence were at the core of prayer. Even the ubiquitous evangelical quiet time seems to verify the essential place of silence in our faith. But finding true silence requires more than quieting our surroundings. It also means quieting our souls. This is the real dilemma of living in a wordy world. Even when we are still and alone, like the minutes before falling asleep in bed, our minds are racing with the images and words we've marinated in all day. It is inner silence that eludes us.

The interior clamor explains why so many people find silence uncomfortable. As Nouwen explains, "One of our main problems is that in this chatty society, silence has become a very fearful thing. For most people, silence creates itchiness and nervousness."[2] As a result we've been conditioned to avoid silence at all costs lest we be confronted with our own inner chaos. We manage to drown out the interior noise of our souls with the exterior noise of our world. And where there is no exterior noise we feverishly work to produce it. In our consumer culture silence is an unholy vacuum that must be filled. Even Christians, betraying their spiritual heritage, are eager to fill silence—albeit with endless words about God.

The Old Testament book of Job illustrates the danger of filling our lives with too many words, even words about God. The book poetically tells the story of a righteous man who loses his family, his fortune, and his health. Job is tormented as he tries to understand the reason behind the calamities that have befallen him. The great majority of the book's forty-two chapters are occupied by Job and his friends conversing definitively about God. They each presume to know the reason behind Job's suffering and to have unqualified insight into the ways of the Lord.

Finally, in chapter thirty-eight, God himself appears to Job in a whirl-wind. "Who is this that darkens counsel by words without knowledge?" the Lord inquires. "Dress for action like a man; I will question you."[3] He proceeds to drill Job with rhetorical questions, with the intent of revealing the chasm between God's knowledge and his. "Where were you when I laid the foundation of the earth?" "Do you know the ordinances of the heavens?" "Can you send forth lightning?" These are just a few of the dozens of questions volleyed at Job. At the end of the sovereign soliloquy, God commands Job to answer.

"Behold," replies Job, "I am of small account; what shall I answer you? I lay my hand on my mouth."[4] After all of his definitive words about God, Job has nothing to say. "I have uttered what I did not understand, things too wonderful for me, which I did not know."[5]

Job learned the wisdom of silence before God, but it appears many Christians have abandoned this value in our wordy world. Perhaps fearing that words about faith will be drowned out if not amplified, in the past decades we have feverishly filled broadcasts, bumpers, billboards, and bookshelves with all kinds of words about God. Apart from expected areas of growth, like the Internet, the past twenty years have seen a steady expansion of Christian radio and television stations as well as print media. In fact, according to George Barna, Christian media has surpassed the church as the source of religious information and experiences for most Americans.[6]

Yes, I recognize the hypocrisy of critiquing the expansion of Christian media while at the same time adding yet another book to the heap. But the problem isn't merely the cacophony of words we are producing about God; it is the nature of those words. Like Job and his companions, our words about God are too often definitive, absolute, and proclaimed with an authority greater than their source. We have a certainty about God and his ways that leads us to replace the mystery of faith with manageable spiritual formulas. In the previous chapter I mentioned our affection for "how to" ministries and three-steps-to-the-solution sermons. Likewise, many have been encouraged to view the Bible primarily as a book of clear-cut answers rather than an ancient book of prophecy, parable, and poetry to be understood contextually. As one teenager in my church said, "Bible stands for *Basic Instructions Before Leaving Earth*." Christian radio is often broadcast with the presumption that God's views are unambiguous, and bestselling Christian books typically include a guaranteed promise of a better marriage, family, job, or life in general. Regardless of the medium, we utter phrases like "God always ...," "God never ...," "God only ...," and even "God hates ..." with flippant regularity. Such absolute pronouncements should rarely be spoken by fallible humans and then only with much trepidation.

The abundance of our definitive words about God shows that we don't view him as a great mystery anymore, but as a sterile calculation without ambiguity or obscurity. And, not surprisingly, this definitive God usually conforms nicely to our personal desires and politics. The resurgence of the prosperity gospel movement is one sign of this. Quoted in a *Time* article titled "Does God Want You to Be Rich?" television preacher Joyce Meyer says, "Who would want to get in on something where you're miserable, poor, broke and ugly and you just have to muddle through until you get to heaven? I believe God wants to give us nice things."[7] She has a point. Who would want an uncontrollable, mysterious, and holy God when you could have a genie in a Bible? Beyond the name-it-and-claim-it crowd, the desire for a definitive God explains our attraction to book titles like *Ten Prayers God Always Says Yes To*, and why a leading Christian political figure could state authoritatively that "God is pro-war."[8] It seems that God's views on politics, economics, social behavior, finances, entertainment, and every other subject are now crystal clear. One needs only to purchase the right book, tune in to the right radio station, or watch the right preacher on television.

With our endless and unqualified words about God, the awe-inspiring Lord that Job encountered in the whirlwind looks today like a tempest in a teacup—a containable, practical, and manageable deity.

THE DIVINE COMMODITY

How much would you pay for someone's toenail clippings? How about a jar of cockroaches? Maybe a French fry shaped like a Nike "swoosh" logo would motivate you to part with your cash? Each of these items found a buyer on the Internet auction site Ebay. If the success of Ebay has taught us anything it's that people will pay for anything—and sometimes they'll even pay for nothing. Numerous sellers have literally listed "Nothing" for sale on Ebay, and even more inexplicably, people have bid on it. As the company's ads declare, whatever you're looking for you can "find 'it' on Ebay," apparently even if "it" is nothing.

What makes a consumer society possible is the belief that anything can be assigned an economic value and exchanged, even toenails and stale French fries. The act of assigning an exchange value to something converts it into a commodity. As a result, an object's value is not linked directly to what it *is* but what it can be exchanged *for*. For example, in a subsistence economy a farmer values the rice he grows because his family survives by eating it. The rice is valuable because of the nutritional quality inherent to it. But once the farmer grows more than enough rice for survival, he can trade the surplus for tools, clothing, or whatever he needs. The farmer does not value this surplus rice for its rice-ness, but because it can be exchanged. Its value is no longer intrinsic but assigned. It has become a commodity.

Over time as our economic system has demanded more and new sources of capital, things previously believed to be beyond economic exploitation have been commodified. In the Cochabamba region of Bolivia, for example, an American company not only succeeded in privatizing the water supply but, in order to control prices, the company even privatized the collection of rainwater. (An uprising among the poor caused the government to later reverse this decision.) In 1980 the United States Patent and Trademark Office overturned a long-standing policy and began allowing corporations to patent living organisms. Today, some estimate that 20 percent of human genes have been patented by corporations and universities. The ability to examine, test, and commercially exploit one fifth of your genetic code is now the exclusive right of someone else. In our modern world the rain that falls freely from the heavens and the molecular building blocks of life have become commodities.

Like so many elements of our consumer culture, commodification is not the problem but rather its pervasiveness. In a commodity culture we have been conditioned to believe nothing carries intrinsic value. Instead, value is found only in a thing's usefulness to us, and tragically this belief has been applied to people as well. Divorce rates have skyrocketed as we've come to see marriage as disposable. When a spouse is no longer useful he or she can be abandoned or traded. Abortion, the termination of an "unwanted" pregnancy, is believed to be morally justifiable because an unborn child is not a person. Personhood is a legal status reserved for those who are deemed useful. Pornography, prostitution, and child sex trafficking are the result of sexuality being commodified. Modern people may express outrage at the horrors of the African slave trade or the Holocaust, but in truth the commodification of human beings that made those atrocities possible is more prevalent today than ever before.

The reduction of even sacred things into commodities also explains why we exhibit so little reverence for God. In a consumer worldview he has no intrinsic value apart from his usefulness to us. He is a tool we employ, a force we control, and a resource we plunder. We ascribe value to him (the literal meaning of the word "worship") based not on who he is, but on what he can do for us.

Christian Smith is a sociologist of religion at the University of Notre Dame. After five years of researching the spiritual lives of American teens he concluded that the faith of most teenagers, including the majority of those who attend churches, is MTD: Moralistic Therapeutic Deism. Smith explains:

> By "moralistic" I mean being good and nice.... By "therapeutic" I mean being primarily concerned with one's own happiness in contrast to focusing on glorifying God, learning obedience, or serving others. Finally, by "deism" I mean a view of God as normally distant and not involved in one's life, except if one has a problem one needs God to solve. In other words, God functions as a combination divine butler and cosmic therapist.[9]

Smith concluded that most teenagers hold this self-centered perception of God because it is the faith most American adults have as well.

Commodification has led most people to view God as a device to be used rather than an all-powerful Creator to be revered. This also explains our abundant and careless words about him. Is it any surprise that a divine butler would fail to provoke reverent silence? What need is there to rein in one's tongue if God is merely a cosmic therapist? The god of Consumer Christianity does not inspire awe and wonder because he is nothing more than a commodity to be used for our personal satisfaction and self-achievement.

OUT OF CONTEXT

How do they do that? I thought to myself as the teenagers' thumbs pecked at their cell phones at lightning speed. I was standing in line at the Gap to return a thoughtful but poor-fitting Christmas gift. The four teens in line ahead of me epitomized the difference between their generation and mine—all four were text messaging on their phones. Culture watchers call them the "Thumb Generation," perpetually connected to the world via digital devices they navigate with their opposable appendages.

One scruffy teenager in line was particularly noteworthy. Gravity seemed to have an additional affect on him. His clothes sagged on his skinny frame as if they were water logged. Even his hair seemed heavy on his face. I wondered how he could see the tiny display on the phone while he texted. White wires emerged from under his hair just enough before they disappeared into the folds of his clothing to give away the presence of an iPod located somewhere on his body. Unless he could smell me staring, I didn't have to worry about being discrete—his senses were sealed off in a digital cocoon. The other techno-teens in line all followed this same pattern to varying degrees. They may have been digitally connected to the world, but they were oblivious to anyone around them.

Connected yet alienated—that is the paradox of our global digital culture. We have access to so many things, yet we are increasingly incapable of seeing those things, or ourselves, in any meaningful context.

To pass the time, I looked at the tags on the clothing I had in my bag. A sweater made in Thailand, a shirt made in Sri Lanka, a pair of pants from Guatemala. My memory retreated to my trip six months earlier to Cambodia. Driving through the outskirts of Phnom Penh, I saw countless identical factories lining the street, each secured behind a brick wall and iron gate.

"What are these?" I asked David, my missionary host for the day.

"Garment factories," he answered. "Clothing is one of the largest industries in Cambodia. Labor is so cheap that most of the brands you buy were probably made here at one time or another. Wal-Mart, Banana Republic, Gap—you name it."

The roadside near some factories was a flurry of activity with merchants selling food to workers, but other factory gates saw no action at all. "It looks like some of them are closed," I said.

"Yeah, that's the crazy part. These American companies will come in, build a multi-million dollar factory, manufacture clothes for one year maybe two, and then some other government will give them a better labor deal, and overnight they'll abandon the factory in Cambodia and start again someplace else."

"Isn't that expensive? I mean, building new factories all the time," I said.

"Are you kidding?" David said, shaking his head. "They make so much profit they don't care. Some of these companies have built and then abandoned factories in Cambodia five or six times."

After miles of clothing factories we drove through a small commercial district crammed with open-air restaurants, shops, and bars. It reminded me of a Western frontier town with mopeds lining the hitching posts rather than horses, and trash blowing across the dirt road rather than tumbleweed.

"This looks like a popular stop," I said.

"Mostly bars and brothels," David said. "Girls from the countryside come to the city to work at the factories. When they shut down, many of the girls become prostitutes. It's the only option they have left. Seeing this will help you understand the work we're doing at our village."

David's village was an hour outside the city amid irrigated rice fields and palm trees. The cluster of eight thatch roof huts had no electricity and shared one well and an ingenious methane stove powered by the manure of two village pigs. The well and stove were built by the missionaries as was the orphanage a short walk from the huts.

As we arrived David explained that every adult in the village had HIV/ AIDS. "The men will travel to the city to sell their crops. They also visit the brothels, contract the virus, and then bring it home and infect their wives. They're not educated and they don't understand how HIV is transmitted." David and his colleagues have made it their mission to educate the village, get medicines, comfort each person as they succumb to the disease, and then care for the children in the orphanage after both their parents are gone.

In one hut a woman on a cot lay dying in the final stages of the disease, open sores on her face and shoulders. Her young daughter, the same age as mine, was being held by a friend in the doorway. The women cried as she held my hand. "Pray for me," she said through David's translation. "Pray for my daughter." Her husband had died the previous month. A few days later, after the mother's cremation, the little girl moved into the orphanage.

After reading the tags on my clothes—Thailand, Sri Lanka, Guatemala—I looked at the text messaging teenagers again. We are so connected. We are so alienated.

CONVENIENT AMNESIA

Recently an economics professor in South Carolina was charged with fraud after the FBI discovered $134 million dollars missing from the investment fund he managed. When the professor was contacted by the Securities and Exchange Commission about the discrepancy, he reported feeling dizzy and checked himself into the hospital with self-diagnosed amnesia.[10] Sometimes amnesia can be very convenient. Without awareness of one's story or context a person can be whomever and whatever he or she desires with no worry of repercussion. Without context there is no responsibility.

After commodification the second unavoidable force of consumerism is alienation. This occurs when a product is disconnected in our mind from the means of its production—from its context. In a sense, we have amnesia toward the things we buy. We can casually browse the racks at the Gap without any thought to the workers who manufactured the clothing. We are oblivious to the factory conditions, the workers' poverty, families, or health. Instead, as we peruse the store we are conditioned to think only about our desires. *Will those pants make me look fat? Is that purse in style? Can that shirt work with my jacket?* We are deluded into believing the items we purchase had no story before they appeared at the store. They exist simply to meet our desire.

Of course, this is not how it has always been. There was a time when an item had value not simply because of its usefulness but because of its context. In a pre-industrial society a chair's worth was found not only in its comfort and fashion but in the fact that Uncle Henry made it. The corn was valuable because you knew the people who planted, harvested, and prepared it. An old pair of shoes were repaired rather than replaced because your children played with the kids of the immigrant man who ran the shoe repair store in town. In the past, everything had a story, and the context of an item contributed to its value just as much, if not more, than one's personal desire. Food, clothing, tools, and virtually everything else people used had a recognized and affirmed relationship to their world. As a result, peoples' responsibility toward the goods they consumed went beyond their immediate usefulness.

In the modern world, however, recognizing the context of the goods we use every day is increasingly difficult. This alienation is reinforced thousands of times whenever we go shopping. Pushing our cart down the aisle at the supermarket we are bombarded with colorful packages. These items are rarely packaged to convey the story of their creation or the human lives impacted by their production. Instead the packaging reinforces our consumer amnesia by appealing only to our desires. Marketing actively discourages shoppers from contemplating where items come from, nor do we want to. We simply want to buy them, use them, enjoy them, and discard them with no larger responsibility.

It should not surprise us that this same pattern, reinforced in our minds since early childhood, should also impact our understanding of God. He too has been alienated from the story that reveals and contextualizes his value. For decades church leaders have been decrying the growing problem of biblical illiteracy among Christians, but the outcries have done little to reverse the trend. Donald Bastian, a Methodist bishop, began noticing an absence of Scripture reading in worship services. Bastian inquired about this trend and reports, "I was told that our worship services should be designed with seekers in mind, and that unchurched people have neither the attention span nor the interest to give to the reading of Bible passages. The idea was that you had to give them a contemporary and, above all, relevant service."[11]

Alienation has conditioned consumers, including the religious variety, to believe context is irrelevant. Value is found only in something's immediate usefulness, in its ability to satisfy our immediate desire. As a result, we have alienated God from the larger story of Scripture that informs us of his character and attributes. At the same time that we are flippantly producing more words about God, we are paradoxically less interested in the words he has spoken about himself. Why bother reading what happened long ago in a land far away? Instead, just boil the story down to three applications on a PowerPoint slide.

This is the view of God a consumer culture feeds to our imaginations—a controllable and convenient deity devoid of any relevant context. But before this false god can be replaced in our minds it must first be erased, shattered by an encounter with the true God beyond our grasp.

FEEL THE INFINITE

Van Gogh's *Starry Night* is one of the most recognizable paintings in the world. This is largely due to the fact that it has been reproduced on countless coffee mugs, T-shirts, and calendars. Of course, this outcome never entered Vincent's imagination when he painted the scene in 1889. Rather, many art historians believe the painting is the pinnacle of van Gogh's spiritual self-expression, his attempt to portray the infinite with swirling strokes of color and light. But our consumer culture cannot resist the urge to trivialize the transcendent. So, like God himself, van Gogh's depiction of the holy has not escaped commodification. Still, by exploring Vincent's original intent for *Starry Night* we may discover a path toward rediscovering the wonder and immensity of God that has been reduced by our culture.

Starry Night was not a hasty production like so many of the canvases van Gogh churned out late in his life. The idea of painting a night landscape seems to have preoccupied the artist for some time and the core elements of the composition—the indigo sky, bright stars, and fire-like cypress tree—were practiced in other paintings before being brought together in *Starry Night*. In fact, referring to a portrait he painted Vincent said, "Instead of painting the ordinary wall of the mean room, I painted infinity, a plain background of the richest, intensest blue that I can contrive, and by this simple combination of the bright head against the rich blue background, I get a mysterious effect, like a star in the depths of an azure sky."[12] Once again choosing to communicate with color, Vincent used blue to symbolize infinity, and the infinite was something he deeply desired. A year before painting *Starry Night* van Gogh wrote to a fellow artist: "I am still charmed by the magic of hosts of memories of the past, of a longing for the infinite, of which the sower, the sheaf are the symbols —just as much as before. But when shall I paint my starry night, that picture which preoccupies me continuously?"[13]

Vincent's "longing for the infinite" predates his artistic period in the south of France. As a younger man his fascination with the natural world often drew him away from his studies. He enjoyed a hike through the hills or meandering on the beach to contemplate the vastness of the ocean. Creation offered van Gogh a sense of communion with God, an experience of the Infinite One that both freed and fed his soul. During his short tenure as a missionary in the Borinage region of Belgium, one villager recalled the lengths to which Vincent would go to experience God's power: "On a very hot day a violent thunderstorm burst over our region. What did our friend do? He went out to stand in the open field to look at the great marvels of God, and so he came back wet to the skin."[14]

But van Gogh's vision of God was not myopic. He not only saw the Infinite in storms and stars, but also in the ordinary:

> When one is in a somber mood, how good it is to walk on the barren beach and look at the grayish-green sea with the long white streaks of the waves. But if one feels the need of something grand, something infinite, something that makes one feel aware of God, one need not go far to find it. I think I see something deeper, more infinite, more eternal than the ocean in the expression of the eyes of a little baby when it wakes in the morning, and coos and laughs because it sees the sun shining on its cradle. If there is a "ray from on high," perhaps one can find it there.[15]

Nonetheless, it was a star-filled sky that captured Vincent's imagination; this was the scene that he longed to paint. The reason may be attributed to Jean-Francois Millet, one of Vincent's favorite artists. Twenty years earlier Millet had painted his own *Starry Night*, a painting van Gogh likely saw during his time in Paris. A biography of Millet written by Alfred Sensier was known to be one of van Gogh's most beloved books. In it he read about his hero's interest in the night sky. "Oh, how I wish I could make those who see my work feel the splendors of the night! One ought to be able to make people hear the songs, the silences and murmurings of the air. They should feel the infinite."[16]

Although Vincent had contemplated creating his night sky for years, the circumstances that led him to finally put paint to canvas were troubling. On May 8, 1889, van Gogh, accompanied by a local pastor, took the train from Arles to Saint-Rémy and admitted himself into an asylum. At night Vincent could peer through the bars of his window and see the rolling Alpilles Mountains, the cypress trees in the countryside, and the stars set in their infinite azure background. Feeling trapped by both the confines of the hospital and his disease, van Gogh's desire to feel the infinite—his longing for God—reached a crescendo. This helps explain the energy of his painting. The brushstrokes are vigorous, the cypress tree seems to be grasping for the heavens, and the glory of the stars reverberates through earth and sky like the ripples of a stone dropped into still water. In his most desperate hour, Vincent sought comfort by remembering there is a God far greater than himself, and by viewing his transient pain in the context of eternity.

Our culture has confined our imaginations with an uninspiring vision of God. He's been reduced to a manageable deity of consumable proportions. To break through this trap we need to see beyond our culture; we need to peer through the bars of commodification and alienation and catch a glimpse of a God far larger than our circumstances. Our imaginations can throw off the shackles of consumerism if we start to feel the infinite once again. This requires taking our gaze off the consumable manifestations of God so prevalent today—the music, T-shirts, jewelry, and yes even books that reduce and confine our perception of the Divine—and replacing them with the silent contemplation of what God himself has created. In a culture that insists on making God small, we can counteract the trend by focusing our imaginations on what is big.

How might our perception of God be changed if we turned off the radio station for a few minutes and walked in a thunderstorm? What if we put down the self-help book and gazed at the ocean for an hour? What might we learn about God and ourselves if our Bible study group gathered outside to stare at the stars in silence? Obviously, the created order only reveals a piece of God's nature and character to us, but that piece is foundational. As the apostle Paul says, "For his invisible attributes, namely, his eternal power and divine nature, have been clearly perceived, ever since the creation of the world, in the things that have been made."[17] It is recognizing God's eternality that liberates our minds from their consumer inclination to reduce him to a commodity. But this recognition must be more than intellectual; it must also be emotional. As van Gogh, Millet, and Paul knew, a correct understanding of God begins when we feel the infinite.

Divine Agnosticism

My brother and sister-in-law took me to a concert at the Hollywood Bowl while I was visiting Southern California recently. The renowned outdoor amphitheater is nestled into the hills of Hollywood creating a scenic environment for 18,000 people to enjoy an evening of music under the stars. As the sun was setting, the members of the orchestra began taking their seats in the white band shell. The sound of the musicians tuning their instruments was odd. Screeching strings echoed. Blasts came from the wind section. It was chaotic and unpleasant.

Finally, the conductor emerged from stage left. The audience erupted in applause as he took his position on the conductor's platform. He calmly raised his arms over his noisy orchestra. Silence. The time for tuning their instruments was over. After a few moments of quiet anticipation, the conductor's arms moved and the soul-stirring music began.

Like an orchestra tuning their instruments, Consumer Christianity is producing chaotic and unpleasant noise about God. The prevailing view of God as an alienated commodity has fueled endless pontificating about his ways and character. This noise reveals a failure of reverence toward the One who declared, "My thoughts are not your thoughts, neither are your ways my ways ... for as the heavens are higher than the earth, so are my ways higher than your ways and my thoughts than your thoughts."[18]

Rather than adding to the noise, perhaps it is time for us to finally be silent, be still, and wait in quiet anticipation for God to begin a new work. Leopold Stokowski, the composer who founded the Hollywood Bowl Orchestra in 1945, once said, "A painter paints his pictures on canvas. But musicians paint their pictures on silence."[19] Maybe God is waiting for us to be silent long enough so he may begin painting a new picture in our imaginations, to begin transforming our image of a manageable deity into one that can truly inspire.

To start reversing our malformed view of God, perhaps we need to cover our mouths with our hands and humbly confess our ignorance, as did Job: "I have uttered what I did not know." Strangely, our first step beyond Consumer Christianity may be toward agnosticism. An agnostic is literally someone who says "I don't know." The word comes from the Greek *a-gnostos* meaning "not-knowing." It is commonly used to mean one who neither affirms nor denies the existence of God. Divine agnosticism, the sort I'm advocating, differs in that it affirms the existence of God but then acknowledges our human inability to fully grasp his infinite nature. Does this mean we can know nothing about God apart from his existence? Of course not. But there is an important hierarchy to knowing; before we can know anything about God we must first humbly confess that we know nothing. Divine agnosticism simply recognizes what Kierkegaard called the "infinite qualitative difference" between God and man. Like Job, an honest relationship with God begins when we accept our finite condition as a creature and cease our futile attempts to contain God with our noisy words.

Job's humble silence before the grandeur of the Almighty was not an isolated event. The same human response has been recorded numerous times in both Scripture and history. Thomas Aquinas was one of the greatest theologians of the Middle Ages. His *Summa Theologica*, which addresses ten thousand objections to the Christian faith, has been called by some one of the greatest intellectual achievements of Western civilization. But on December 6, 1273, Aquinas abruptly announced to his secretary that he would write no more. While worshiping in the chapel of Saint Nicholas, Aquinas had an intense experience with God. "I can do no more," he said, "such things have been revealed to me that all I have written seems to me as so much straw."[20]

More recently, Karl Barth, arguably the twentieth century's most celebrated and prolific theologian, also came to recognize the inadequacy of his words about God. Barth envisioned entering heaven pushing a cart full of his books and hearing the angels laugh. He said, "In heaven we shall know all that is necessary, and we shall not have to write on paper or read more.... Indeed, I shall be able to dump even the *Church Dogmatics*, over the growth of which the angels have long been amazed, on some heavenly floor as a pile of waste paper."[21]

Consumerism, with its never-ending noise about its consumable god, has led us to believe that our words and notions about God are of supreme importance. It has made the church into a noisy orchestra without harmony and fearful of silence. But humble silence offers us liberation from our digital cocoons to experience wonder once again. Silence allows us the space to contemplate the vastness of the heavens and the God beyond them. Silence can shatter the trivialized deity that has occupied our imaginations and provide God the canvas to begin a new work in our souls.

CHAPTER 3

BRANDING OF THE HEART

*The more I think about it, the more I realize there is
nothing more artistic than to love others.*

Vincent van Gogh

IT'S GOTTA BE THE SHOES

Seventeen-year-old Steve Terrett left his southside Chicago home around
9:00 p.m. to visit a girl. He was wearing his new Nike Air Jordan "Solid-
ify" shoes—a $110 gift from his mother. Steve always insisted on wearing
the latest fashions. The white leather shoes with blue streaks were certainly
eye-catching, but it was the logo of Chicago Bulls legend Michael Jordan
near the ankle—a silhouette of Jordan with legs spread soaring with a
basketball—that made the shoes truly fashionable. One fan described the
logo as "an almost angelic symbol: Sport mixed with divinity." That seems
fitting for gym shoes said to evoke "something larger than athletics, and
perhaps life itself."[1]

I wonder if Steve Terrett thought his shoes were worth more than life
itself when police found him in an alley at 10:30 p.m., a bullet in his back.
He told the officers two teenagers had "set him up" for his Air Jordan
shoes. He died later that night.[2]

Steve Terrett was the latest teenager to join the ranks of those murdered for their athletic footwear. Shortly after Nike debuted the Air Jordan
brand in 1985, stories began circulating about kids being killed for the
sneakers. Amazingly, the reports of violence only increased the mythic status of the shoes initially created by advertisers. It was the kind of publicity
Nike could not buy, and the company continues to profit from it twenty
years later. Consider that the same week Steve Terrett was murdered for his
shoes in Chicago, a few miles away consumers waited in line for three days

47

outside the Niketown store on Michigan Avenue for a chance to purchase the brand's newest release.

What would motivate someone to murder another human being for a pair of shoes? That is a rational question that never entered my adolescent mind or those of my prepubescent friends. Instead we begged our parents to shell out $100 for a pair of Air Jordans, believing survival in junior high depended on it. Although these emotional tactics were unsuccessful on my parents, it was still a memorable day when any boy walked into class with a new pair of Air Jordans. With his blue jeans tightly rolled up around the ankle so the high-tops were fully exposed, everyone took notice. The wearer expected our homage, and he received it. After all, these were no ordinary sneakers. The shoes with Michael Jordan's angelic logo soaring through the air were worthy of worship and even blood sacrifice.

One child sacrificed on Nike's altar was fifteen-year-old Michael Thomas. His grandmother warned him about wearing the shoes to school. "We said somebody might like them, and he said, 'Granny, before I let anyone take those shoes, they'll have to kill me.'" Two weeks later he was strangled by his seventeen-year-old basketball buddy for his shoes.

Shortly after, a journalist handed Michael Jordan a news report of the murder. Jordan happened to be wearing the same Nikes that cost Michael Thomas his life. He silently read the article. "I can't believe it," Jordan said somberly. "Choked to death. By his friend." After sighing Jordan asked if there had been other kids murdered for shoes branded with his image. "Yes," he was told. "Plenty."

Shaking his head Jordan said, "I never thought because of endorsement of a shoe, or any product, that people would harm each other. Everyone likes to be admired, but when it comes to kids actually killing each other" — he paused — "then you have to reevaluate things."[3]

SELLING THE SIZZLE

British entrepreneur Richard Branson opened his first Virgin record store on Oxford Street in London in 1971. Today the Virgin empire includes airlines, soft drinks, comic books, mobile phones, even wedding gowns and spacecraft. There are over 350 companies imprinted with the Virgin logo generating more than $20 billion in revenue. "In the beginning," says Branson, "it was just about the business — now it's about the brand." "Branding is everything."[4]

More than a name or logo, a brand is a manufactured idea that infiltrates the imagination. Colin Bates, a marketing expert, says "a brand is a collection of perceptions in the mind of the consumer."[5] As such, the goal of branding is not the development of an eye-catching logo. The goal of branding is to manipulate peoples' minds so they involuntarily associate that logo with predetermined feelings, or as Nike states in its corporate mission statement: "To nurture relevant emotional ties between the Nike brand and consumer segments."[6] Nurturing emotional ties is not a process that targets the logical faculties of the brain. Instead, branding is a more artistic endeavor that relies heavily on the mind's imaginative power.

There is nothing inherently luxurious about a three-pointed star in a circle, but when consumers see a Mercedes-Benz logo their brains have been programmed to instantly associate it with status. It is by design that Walt Disney's scripted autograph immediately brings to mind "family" and "fun" in the collective American imagination. And when a brand becomes tainted in our minds it must be reborn. In 1996, a ValuJet flight departing from Miami plunged into the Everglades. The low-cost airline, plagued by quality and safety concerns, lost $55 million and was near bankruptcy. A year later, ValuJet rebranded itself as AirTran. Passengers did not associate the new brand with poor safety, and the company soared back to profitability.

The most successful brands have legitimized the notion that image is everything. The McDonald's brand, for example, has been so effectively imprinted onto our imaginations that a recent Stanford University study found carrots, milk, and apple juice tasted better to children when they were packaged in McDonald's wrappers. Dr. Tom Robinson, who headed the study, said the children's sense of taste was "physically altered by the branding."[7] By creating emotional connections to the McDonald's brand in children's minds, advertisers have been able to alter their perception of reality and their behavior. Given the choice, children will select the food served in a McDonald's wrapper every time. This is why Colin Bates says, "A brand is the most valuable real estate in the world, a corner of the consumer's mind."[8]

When Sir Richard Branson says his business is "all about the brand" he means targeting a corner of the consumer's mind and filling it with positive feelings about Virgin. Once this mental real estate is owned and occupied, the brand's logo can be slapped on virtually anything, and the consumer will be positively predisposed toward it. This represents a significant shift in the way businesses understand themselves. In the past, winning a consumer's money required developing a quality product that met a real need, but today companies are increasingly focused on a product's branding rather than its substance. "This allows companies to produce cheaper and cheaper products under the same brand image, because people are buying the cachet, image, or identity associated with the brand as much as—or more than—the quality of the product itself."[9] In other words, corporations have learned it's more effective to sell the sizzle than the steak.

Consider coffee. Former vice-president of marketing for Starbucks, Scott Bedbury, confesses that "consumers don't truly believe there's a huge difference between products," so to sell a $4 cup of coffee the real goal is "to establish emotional ties."[10] Howard Schultz, the founder of Starbucks, says what his company actually sells is "the romance of the coffee experience, the feeling of warmth and community people get in Starbucks stores."[11] Phil Knight, founding CEO of Nike, affirms the perspective stated by leaders at Starbucks and Virgin. "For years we thought of ourselves as a production-oriented company, meaning we put all our emphasis on designing and manufacturing the products. But now we understand the most important thing we do is market the product.... Nike is a marketing-oriented company."[12]

Consumerism has created a culture that values style over substance, image over reality, and perception over performance. Naomi Klein, in her fascinating book *No Logo*, shows how this approach reached maturity by the 1990s. "'Brands, not products!' became the rallying cry for a marketing renaissance led by a new breed of companies that saw themselves as 'meaning brokers' instead of product producers."[13] Successful companies finally discovered what philosopher Jean Baudrillard had known for decades: "Consumption is a system of meaning."[14] We define our identity and construct meaning for our lives through the brands we consume.

The most blatant example of branding-as-identity in recent memory may be the popular Mac verses PC ad campaign produced by Apple. The commercials feature a trendy, comfortable young man who unpretentiously introduces himself, "Hi, I'm a Mac." Standing to his right is a pudgy, middle-aged man in an outdated suit. He stiffly says, "I'm a PC." The message could not be clearer. Purchasing the Apple brand means you are young, hip, and friendly. In the viewer's imagination the message is not about computers but identity. Even Bill Gates, chairman of Microsoft, makes this mental leap when commenting about the ads in a *Newsweek* interview. He says, "I don't think the over 90 percent of the [population] who use Windows PCs think of themselves as dullards, or the kind of klutzes that somebody is trying to say they are."[15] Nothing in the commercials explicitly communicates PC *users* are dullards or klutzes, but that is the power of branding. It triggers the imaginative ability of the mind to make these associations automatically. Branding has allowed Apple to become a seller of identity and not merely computers.

The link between brands and self-identity helps explain, at least in part, why young men will murder each other for a pair of gym shoes. Lieutenant Thomas Malacek, a police officer investigating one such crime, said, "It's becoming a growing problem, because apparently these items have a lot more identity value than in the past."[16] Branding has linked certain shoes with power, success, and status in our minds. But, as sociologist Elijah Anderson notes, many urban youth lack the educational and professional opportunities to legitimately add these qualities to their identity. Instead, "they value these 'emblems,' these symbols of supposed success. The gold, the shoes, the drug dealer's outfit."[17] As a result, it isn't the economic value of the sneakers that drives someone to kill, it's the identity associated with a particular brand. Perhaps this is what Nike means by "nurturing relevant emotional ties between the Nike brand and the consumer." After all, no one has been murdered for a pair of Keds.

A IS FOR APPLE

I took the morning off to walk my daughter to her first day of kindergarten. My wife, pushing our son in his stroller, was holding back her tears. Zoe, on the other hand, was genuinely excited as she skipped down the sidewalk with her oversized pink backpack reaching to her knees, and her black hair flipping across her shoulders. *What new experiences awaited her?* I wondered as my own kindergarten memories returned. There was snack time with animal crackers and milk. Of course, Erica Lewis had orange juice due to her milk allergy. And letter time on the carpet where I always sat next to Brian Carlson with our little chalkboard tablets copying the alphabet. And I'll never forget Bob Grout, infamous for removing his glass eye, putting it in his mouth, and chasing the girls around the classroom. Kindergarten was great. I found myself both excited for Zoe and jealous.

Outside the school the five-year-olds lined up along the fence preparing for the teacher to lead them inside. They looked like soldiers going off to war—tears and kisses and last-second "I love you's" were lofted across the playground. The bell rang and the kindergarten battalion marched away. A parade of colorful backpacks—Spiderman, Barbie, Buzz Lightyear, Strawberry Shortcake, X-Men, and My Little Pony—disappeared one by one through the door, and the parents were left alone to console one another. *Would they make it? Would they survive?*

Three hours later we gathered again as our little soldiers came zipping out the door. "Daddy, Daddy! Guess what?" Zoe said as she ran into my arms. "I got my first homework assignment!" I knew in a few years she wouldn't be as excited.

"Homework," I said, "in kindergarten?" I gave my wife a confused glance. "I guess things have changed since we were kids." Zoe eagerly pulled the paper from her backpack. It read:

> Dear Parents,
>
> Here is your child's first kindergarten "homework"! Please help your child find "logos" such as the ones displayed on this page to help reinforce the concept that he/she can already read! They may be on bags, boxes, cups, cans, etc. The children feel great about their ability to read them. We will use them for sharing and also to create a display in our classroom. Thanks for helping!!!

I asked Zoe if she could "read" any of the logos on the paper. Without hesitating she identified Pizza Hut, Target, and Lego. At home she collected the logos of Disney, Jewel (our local supermarket), Jell-O, and Goldfish Crackers. Later, while drinking a glass of water, she proudly shouted, "That says IKEA!" She spotted the tiny logo imprinted on the bottom of the glass.

When I was in kindergarten we learned the alphabet by associating letters with generic objects. A is for apple. B is for ball. C is for cat. Zoe's first step toward reading is identifying corporate brands. A is for Apple Computer. B is for Burger King. C is for Cheerios. Should it scare me that my five-year-old has memorized more corporate brands than prayers, Bible verses, or even names of relatives? Also scary is the fact that no one taught her to identify logos. We don't have logo flashcard drills at home. Zoe has internalized these logos simply by living for five years in a brand-saturated culture, and now they'll be posted on the bulletin board in her classroom too.

In truth, I should not be surprised that my kindergartener is already brand savvy. As marketers have discovered the power of branding on the imagination, they have become eager to target the malleable imaginations of children, the segment of the population with the least defined self-identity and a willingness to shift their identity without reflection. By choosing a My Little Pony or Superman backpack, Zoe and her classmates are already learning to build their identities with brands, and this process will continue the remainder of their lives. Why else would companies like Ford and Pizza Hut spend millions of dollars marketing in preschools?[18] Three- and four-year-olds cannot order a pizza or buy a car, but by planting a branded seed in the kids' imaginations and associating it with positive feelings, these corporations hope to reap the fruit when these children begin to form their identities as teenagers. This sort of brand marketing has been so effective that the average ten-year-old has already memorized between 300 and 400 brands. When these children become adolescents, each with an average of $100 of disposable cash to spend every week, they will select from these brands to construct their identities—identities they can eat, drink, smoke, drive, play, ride, and wear.

The link between brands and identity helps explain a new trend uncovered by Cleveland Evans, a psychology professor at Nebraska's Bellevue University. After studying recent Social Security records he's reported an increase in the number of children named after popular brands. Decades from now, when Zoe's first child lines up for her first day of kindergarten she may be standing in line with Infiniti, Celica, Armani, Timberland, Nautica, L'Oreal, or ESPN.[19] I only hope my granddaughter isn't named IKEA.

FROM LORD TO LABEL

The identity-forming power of brands means the act of shopping has immense significance in a consumer culture. As Benjamin Barber writes, "If brand names can shape or even stand in for identity, then to figure out 'who you are' you must decide where (and for what) you shop."[20] This may explain why shopping is now the number one leisure activity for Americans. As we peruse the shopping mall we are not simply looking for a sweater, a computer, or a backpack—we are looking for ourselves. Shopping occupies a role in society that once belonged only to religion—the power to give meaning and construct identity. "To shop," as Pete Ward observes, "is to seek for something beyond ourselves" and this desire "indicates a spiritual inclination in many of the everyday activities of shopping."[21]

The spiritual and religious importance of shopping in a consumer culture is not lost on marketers. Douglas Atkin, author of *The Culting of Brands: When Customers Become True Believers*, states plainly that, "Brands are the new religion." They "supply our modern metaphysics, imbuing the world with significance.... Brands function as complete meaning systems."[22] Because brands have a power over us on par with religion, Atkin believes "cults are a rich and legitimate source of insight for the creation of brand worship."[23] The spiritual, even cultic, ability of brands to construct self-identity is described by Marty Neumeier this way:

> Depending on your Unique Buying State, you can join any number of tribes on any number of days and feel part of something bigger than yourself. You can belong to the Callaway tribe when you play golf, the VW tribe when you drive to work, and the Williams-Sonoma tribe when you cook a meal. You're part of a select clan (or so you feel) when you buy products from these clearly differentiated companies. Brands are the little gods of modern life, each ruling a different need, activity, mood, or situation. Yet you're in control. If your latest god falls from Olympus, you can switch to another one.[24]

If brands are the new religion, is the opposite also true? Have religions been reduced to brands? The evidence suggests they have. As outlined in chapter one, researchers are not able to differentiate the behaviors and values of self-identified Christians from non-Christians with one exception — what they buy. As total sales of religious products reaches $7 billion annually, it appears that God's people are constructing and expressing their identity through the consumption of Christ-branded products. As Mark Riddle observes, "Conversion in the U.S. seems to mean we've exchanged some of our shopping at Wal-Mart, Blockbuster, and Borders for the Christian Bookstore down the street. We've taken our lack of purchasing control to God's store, where we buy our office supplies in Jesus' name."[25]

According to Pete Ward, the use of brands by Christians to construct identity accounts for the wild success of the WWJD bracelets. "For many of these younger teenagers identity is uniquely invested in the purchase and display of products. These products act as symbols within a wider meaning system. WWJD managed to incarnate Christ inside this fairly arid world, and it did so by commodification."[26] Ward endorses Christian-branded products as a legitimate way to "incarnate Christ" in our culture. But based on this logic it appears the apostle John got the opening words of his gospel wrong. The Word did not need to be made flesh. The Word (literally "logo" in Greek) simply needed to be branded onto popular merchandise. In a consumer culture "incarnating Christ" no longer carries an expectation of Christians loving God and their neighbors, but rather the perpetual consumption of Christian merchandise — music, books, T-shirts, gifts, and jewelry. A person's identity as a Christian has less to do with internally transformed values, and more to do with externally displayed products.

Paralleling the corporate shift away from manufacturing goods to manufacturing brands, Christianity in North America has drifted from a faith of substance to a faith of perception. Consider how people select a church. Two generations ago when denominational loyalty was high, a church was chosen primarily based on the doctrinal beliefs it espoused. Today, the music style used in worship is the issue of paramount importance when choosing a church. Rick Warren, pastor of Saddleback Church, says, "Music may be the most influential factor in determining who your church reaches for Christ, and whether or not your church grows."[27] Like Virgin, Nike, and Starbucks, the church has learned that success in a consumer culture has more to do with the packaging than the product. It's more about the sizzle than the steak.

This emphasis on style over substance is at work at the individual level as well. In a culture where people construct identity by consuming brands, we should not be surprised that Jesus-branded clothing lines are proliferating. 1in3Trinity is one example. Started by a former merchandising executive, the 1in3Trinity brand includes clothing for men and women as well as an energy drink "fused with the Fruit of the Spirit." The company's website says, "The 1in3Trinity lifestyle brand of clothing and accessories is created to strengthen and sustain Christians in their walk." And adds, "It's not only about wearing your faith on your sleeve; it's much more! It's about living day to day, trying your best to be a great example of God's love."[28]

The marketing effort tells Christian consumers that branding oneself with 1in3Trinity merchandise is a way of both expressing and strengthening their inner Christian identity. But elsewhere on the website the company deconstructs the existence of any qualitative distinction between Christians and non-Christians. "We want to share with you what it means to us to be a Christian," the company declares. "When we say 'We're a Christian,' we are not shouting we are righteous. We are whispering we are lost ... we are admitting we often fall like many and need Christ to pick us up.... We are not claiming to be perfect ... we are not 'holier than thou.' We are just simple sinners who received God's gifts of love, grace and mercy."[29]

The definition of a Christian espoused by the 1in3Trinity brand echoes a popular bumper sticker: *Christians Aren't Perfect, Just Forgiven.* Responding to this sentiment, Dallas Willard asks, "*Just* forgiven? And is that really all there is to being a Christian?" Willard recognizes the insidious theology behind the slogan—a theology promoted by Consumer Christianity. "It says that you can have a faith in Christ that brings forgiveness, while in every other respect your life is no different from that of others who have no faith in Christ at all."[30]

If being a Christian is not marked by a life of increasing righteousness, holiness, faithfulness, love, or justice, what remains to differentiate a follower of Christ from other people? Perhaps that is the point. If being a Christian involves no internal transformation, then an external transformation will have to suffice—an external transformation provided by "lifestyle brands" like 1in3Trinity. Approaching Christianity as a brand explains why the majority of people who identify themselves as Christians live no differently than other Americans yet spend enormous amounts of money on Christian products. Rather than adopting a biblical worldview, they have simply added a Jesus fish onto the bumper of their consumer identities. And like the products they purchase, the branded Christian's identity will always be more about image than substance.

Circumcise Your Heart

"You want me to do *what* to *where*?" I can just imagine Abraham's reaction when he heard God's commandment. "This is my covenant," the Lord said. "Every male among you shall be circumcised. You shall be circumcised in the flesh of your foreskins, and it shall be a sign of the covenant between me and you."[31] Although circumcision was not an uncommon practice in the ancient Near East, and Abraham was probably familiar with the custom, at ninety-nine years old I'm sure he was not enthusiastic about performing the procedure on himself. Thankfully, later generations of Abraham's descendents would be spared the trauma of self-mutilation. Instead, Jewish boys were circumcised when just eight days old.

It's difficult to overstate the importance of circumcision to the identity of ancient Israelites. It was *the* identifying marker of God's people. In fact, to be uncircumcised was seen as a rejection of one's Jewish identity. Abraham was told that any male not "cut in the flesh of his foreskin" was to be "cut off" from his people. The identity-forming significance of circumcision led to the Hebrew word for "uncircumcised" becoming synonymous with "unclean" or "heathen."[32] Because the absence of a foreskin carried so much meaning in the ancient world, in a real way it was the prototype religious brand — an external marker of one's spiritual identity, a symbol that provoked feelings of national and religious pride in the imaginations of God's people.

So, imagine the shock of his Jewish audience when the apostle Paul wrote, "For neither circumcision counts for anything nor uncircumcision."[33] These were blasphemous words coming from a Jew. After all, Paul himself was a self-described "Hebrew of Hebrews ... circumcised on the eighth day."[34] Why would he reject the most sacred mark of Jewish identification — repeatedly?[35] Why would he tell a community of Christ-followers that "if you accept circumcision, Christ will be of no advantage to you?"[36]

Paul rejected circumcision because he understood that external branding was meaningless if it did not reflect an internal reality. In Romans 2, he argues that *real* circumcision is not outward and physical, but inward and spiritual — "circumcision is a matter of the heart."[37] Paul was referencing three Old Testament passages in which the Lord called his people to circumcise their hearts.[38] God's people, past and present, have exhibited a chronic problem of focusing upon external branding to construct their identity. We have always needed frequent reminders about what matters most — a heart marked and set apart for God.

Paul's vehement opposition to circumcision at the time was in response to Jewish Christians commanding non-Jews to be circumcised if they wished to be followers of Christ. All their lives these Jews had been formed to view their spiritual identity as a matter of external branding, and they were uncritically carrying this perspective into their new identities as Christians. But Paul recognized the danger of this thinking. A focus on external marking (circumcision) would result in the neglect of internal devotion, and this contradicted the intent of God in the old covenant and the teaching of Christ in the new covenant.

We face a similar danger today. We've been shaped all our lives by a consumer culture in which identity is constructed through external brands. We express who we are with the brands we consume. When we become followers of Christ, we can uncritically carry this understanding into our new identity as Christians. There may be nothing sinister at work; we are not intending to undermine Jesus' emphasis on the heart. But our imaginations have been wired to think of identity as an external construction. We harmonize the gospel with this conventional view whenever we express our faith by wearing Christ-branded T-shirts or when we attach a chrome fish to our tailgate. If addressing contemporary consumers, the apostle Paul might rewrite his epistle this way: *For no one is a Christian who is merely one outwardly, nor is branding outward and physical. But a Christian is one inwardly, and branding is a matter of the heart.*

This is not a prohibition against Christian brands. And it's worth noting that, strictly speaking, Paul was not against circumcision. (In fact, he had his companion Timothy circumcised for a pragmatic reason, and he spoke against a practice whereby Jewish men had their circumcision reversed in order to assimilate into Roman society.) Paul's problem was assigning a spiritual significance to an external mark, and he feared his young converts would be stalled in their spiritual growth by conforming to a culture focused on externalities. His goal was to draw their focus off circumcision altogether and toward the heart. He plainly says, "For in Christ Jesus neither circumcision nor uncircumcision counts for anything, but only faith working through love."[39]

Likewise, Christian-branded products count for nothing. They simply don't matter. They cannot contribute to the internal work of Christ in our hearts, and no amount of religious products makes us Christian. However, being immersed in a culture that's wired us to focus on externalities means the avalanche of Jesus-junk marketed at Christians does carry a danger. It tempts us back to conventional thinking, a focus on externalities, and a neglect of the heart. So, if displaying Christ-branded products offers no spiritual benefit, and if they carry a potential for stalling our spiritual growth, wisdom calls us to focus our energies and resources elsewhere.

Rather than putting on a "Tommy Hellfighter" T-shirt, a "Got Jesus?" bumper sticker, or "Jesus Is My Homeboy" underwear,[40] why not follow Paul's advice and focus our energy toward putting on "compassionate hearts, kindness, humility, meekness, and patience."[41] This is how our identity is revealed, not by the brands we display, but by faith working through love. Jesus said, "By this all people will know that you are my disciples, if you have love for one another."[42] Christ's true people are branded with love.

SHIRTS VERSUS SKINS

Before I left for college my high school history teacher gave me a bit of advice. "Just remember one thing and you'll be fine," he said. "College isn't the real world." After arriving on campus I quickly discovered he was right.

A few months into my freshman year at Miami University in Oxford, Ohio, I witnessed a moral battle that bordered on the ludicrous. The Gay, Lesbian, and Bisexual Alliance (GLBA) was sponsoring the annual Gay Pride Week on campus. The festivities included a plywood "closet" positioned in front of the student center from which professors and students would emerge to publicly declare their sexual orientation. There were also benches placed along congested sidewalks where same-sex couples would make out in order to desensitize students to public displays of gay affection. Apart from these publicity stunts, the week did include more meaningful events aimed at education, awareness, and dialogue between people from differing points of view.

The fashion war began when the GLBA posted signs announcing "Jean Day." The flyers invited students to show their support for the GLBA's agenda by wearing denim jeans on Thursday. By selecting jeans, a second skin for most college students, it was obvious the GLBA was seeking to inflate the popularity of its cause. The tactic was so transparent few people paid attention—that is, until a conservative Christian group began putting up their own signs. The Christian flyers, distinguishable by a Jesus-fish logo, called students who *did not* support gay rights to "wear a shirt on Thursday." The battle lines were drawn. The silliness of the GLBA's scheme was matched and surpassed by the stupidity of the Christians'.

Thursday came, and while most students did not participate in the fashion battle, those who did were difficult to miss. Members of the GLBA walked the campus in their blue jeans, the guys shirtless, the women wearing only bras. The conservative Christians marched to class wearing khaki pants and in some cases multiple shirts, proudly doing their part to "uphold righteousness." Despite the silly antics, it appeared Jean Day would be one of peaceful self-expression—that is until Brother Jeb arrived. Jeb was an itinerant street preacher who came through town once or twice a year. He must have amended his itinerary when he heard the hype surrounding Gay Pride Week and the showdown with the Christians. Brother Jeb set up his pulpit, a plastic crate, ten yards from the GLBA's coming-out closet in front of the student center. He stood on the crate and shouted through a bull horn. Hanging from his shoulders a placard painted with flames read:

> Homosexuals
> Lesbians
> Bisexuals
> Effeminates
> Fornicators
> Adulterers
> Abortionists
> Feminists
> **REPENT!**

A crowd soon gathered. Some laughed at Jeb; others were shocked by his venomous words. A few students could be seen crying. Members of the GLBA arrived on the scene and began arguing with Jeb. As the spectacle kept growing, the khaki-wearing Christians were paralyzed. They certainly didn't want to be associated with Brother Jeb, but they couldn't denounce him either. That might be interpreted as supporting the GLBA.

The mad scene was a microcosm of a culture in which everyone "wears" their identity. The gay community displayed their jeans. The conservatives displayed their khakis. Brother Jeb displayed his flaming placards. There was one exception. Positioned between Jeb's pulpit and the GLBA's closet was Dave. I knew Dave because he lived two floors above me in the dorm, and we became good friends early freshman year. Dave stood amid the chaos in front of the student center with a large metal tank strapped to his back. It was a thermos filled with hot chocolate. With a hose from the backpack he filled cups and offered the free drinks to students on their way to witness the battle between Brother Jeb and the GLBA. Occasionally, someone would stop and ask Dave why he was giving away free drinks. "It's just a way of reminding you that God loves you," he would reply.

Dave's ministry was not limited to hot chocolate. The morning after a fraternity party he'd enter the house and begin collecting beer cans and cleaning the bathrooms. In the autumn, he recruited friends to rake the yards of local residents. He washed windshields, handed out popsicles on hot days, and even fed parking meters—something campus security did not appreciate given the revenue generated from parking tickets. Dave never accepted a payment or tip of any kind, and his goal was not to verbally present the gospel or leave behind a tract. He simply wanted to show God's love in tangible ways.

This greatly perplexed both the Christians and non-Christians at Miami. When people discovered the motivation behind Dave's service, some were uncomfortable. Christians, they thought, are prejudiced and belligerent. But how do you disagree with someone who isn't trying to argue? How do you refuse an act of kindness from someone who expects nothing in return? The official Christian groups on campus also didn't know what to do with Dave. When he approached them for funds to expand his work, they denied his request. Apparently Dave was not doing real ministry. By revealing his identity through loving service, rather than external brands, products, or labels, Dave was doing more than perplexing the Miami University campus. He was taking his place in a long line of saints who've raised eyebrows by favoring actions over image.

In the fourth-century, a young Egyptian peasant was abducted and forced into the Roman army. While awaiting transport up the Nile, Pachomius and the other conscripts languished away in a jail. Local Christians arrived with food, water, and other supplies to care for the men. Pachomius was puzzled. He asked who these caregivers were. "They are Christians," he was told.

"What is a Christian?" Pachomius asked.

"They are people who bear the name of Christ, the only begotten Son of God, and they are merciful to everyone, including strangers."[43] How many people would define a Christian that way today?

Pachomius was so amazed by the Christians' actions that he vowed to commit himself to their God if he ever found freedom. When he was discharged shortly thereafter, he sought a local church and was baptized. Pachomius later became one of the leading voices of the early monastic movement.

A more contemporary example comes from war-torn Baghdad. Ghassan Thomas leads one of the few public churches that emerged after Saddam Hussein was toppled. His congregation erected a sign on their building that said "Jesus Is the Light of the World," but the church was raided by bandits who left behind a threat on a piece of cardboard. It read: "Jesus is not the light of the world, Allah is, and you have been warned." The note was signed "The Islamic Shiite Party."

In response, Pastor Ghassan loaded a van with children's gifts and medical supplies—which were in critically short supply following the American invasion—and drove to the headquarters of the Islamic Shiite Party. After presenting the gifts and supplies to the sheikh, Ghassan told the leader, "Christians have love for you, because our God is a God of love." He then asked permission to read from his Bible. Ghassan turned to Jesus' words in John 8, "I am the light of the world." He then showed the cardboard note to the sheikh. The Muslim leader, astounded by Pastor Thomas's actions, apologized.

"This will not happen again," he vowed. "You are my brother. If anyone comes to kill you, it will be my neck first." The sheikh later attended Pastor Thomas's ordination service at the church.[44]

No discussion of incomprehensible love would be complete without mentioning Francis of Assisi, the twelfth-century nobleman turned missionary. Francis was born to a very wealthy family, but after a short career as a soldier and socialite he experienced a dramatic transformation. Inexplicably, he began hugging lepers in the street, giving away his expensive clothing, and associating with the poor. The people of Assisi thought the young man had lost his mind. His father was so embarrassed he took Francis to court in an effort to stop his son's irrational behavior.

His father demanded the return of the money Francis had given to the poor. Francis agreed and immediately began removing his clothes. Standing naked before the court, he handed the clothing to his father and said, "Until now I have called you my father on earth; from now on I desire to say only 'Our Father who art in heaven.'" Francis left the court and began a new life devoted wholly to loving God and loving others.

Maybe that's what we need to do—get naked. We have been fathered by a consumer culture and clothed with branded identities. Perhaps it is time for us to strip away the labels we've been wearing, even the Christian ones, and give them back. Imagine expressing our faith without the clothing, knickknacks, Bible covers, and bumper stickers. Imagine being set free from clever logos and manufactured brands that express an idea of love but are incapable of expressing love itself. What if we began using our God-created and Spirit-filled bodies as instruments of Christ's love, rather than what we attach to them? Pachomius's visitors, Pastor Thomas of Baghdad, Francis of Assisi, my friend Dave, and Jesus all expressed their identities through love—and most people found their actions bewildering.

After discarding his old identity, Francis left Assisi dressed as a beggar. Walking along the road he was attacked by robbers. He told them he was the messenger of a great king. They tagged him as a poor idiot, beat him, and threw him off the road. But the robbers walked away confused when they heard Francis singing praises to God while lying in the snowy ditch.

THE GOOD DUTCHMAN

A lawyer stood up to put [Jesus] to the test, saying, "Teacher, what shall I do to inherit eternal life?" He said to him, "What is written in the Law? How do you read it?" And he answered, "You shall love the Lord your God with all your heart and with all your soul and with all your strength and with all your mind, and your neighbor as yourself." And he said to him, "You have answered correctly; do this, and you will live."

But he, desiring to justify himself, said to Jesus, "And who is my neighbor?" Jesus replied, "A man was going down from Jerusalem to Jericho, and he fell among robbers, who stripped him and beat him and departed, leaving him half dead. Now by chance a priest was going down that road, and when he saw him he passed by on the other side. So likewise a Levite, when he came to the place and saw him, passed by on the other side. But a Samaritan, as he journeyed, came to where he was, and when he saw him, he had compassion. He went to him and bound up his wounds, pouring on oil and wine. Then he set him on his own animal and brought him to an inn and took care of him. And the next day he took out two denarii and gave them to the innkeeper, saying, 'Take care of him, and whatever more you spend, I will repay you when I come back.' Which of these three, do you think, proved to be a neighbor to the man who fell among the robbers?" He said, "The one who showed him mercy." And Jesus said to him, "You go, and do likewise."[45]

In December 1878, Vincent van Gogh arrived in the tiny Belgian village of Petit-Wasmes. He was eager to pursue a career in ministry, and the Dutch Reformed Church supported van Gogh on a six-month trial as an evangelist to the impoverished miners of the region. Upon arriving, Vincent quickly set himself apart from other clergymen. He did not seek to be treated with the usual respect and dignity of a pastor. He rented space in the home of a baker, but soon angered his landlord's wife by cutting up his linens to provide bandages for workers burned in the mines.

Van Gogh's generosity toward the miners extended to his personal affects as well. He arrived at the baker's home one day with no shirt and no socks. He'd given them away. The baker's mother asked, "Monsieur Vincent, why do you deprive yourself of all your clothes like this—you who are descended from such a noble family of Dutch pastors?" He answered, "I am a friend of the poor like Jesus was."[46]

Eventually, van Gogh considered his lodging too luxurious when compared to the filthy homes of the people he was sent to shepherd. So, he left the baker's cottage and took up residence in the smallest hovel in the village. Vincent had no furniture and slept on the ground near the hearth. Seeing the destitution and poverty of the miners, he also gave away most of his clothing and his money. Another pastor recalls van Gogh's lifestyle at the time: "I should add that the cleanliness of the Dutchman was also abandoned. Soap was discarded as a sinful luxury and so if he was not entirely covered by a layer of coal, our evangelist's face was even dirtier than those of the miners. Exterior details did not concern him."[47]

Beyond his generosity and identification with the miners, it was Vincent's compassion that impressed the people. When an explosion in the mine devastated the entire region, Vincent committed himself to caring for the victims with their black, disfigured faces. One man the doctors had given up on was taken in by Vincent, who paid for his care for forty days. The man recovered, and Vincent's neighbors began referring to him as the Good Samaritan. During the strike that followed the accident, the miners only trusted "Le Pasteur Vincent," refusing to listen to anyone else. Van Gogh had won the people with his love, and his mission excelled. Reverend Bonte recalls one of Vincent's conversions:

> People still talk about the miner whom he went to see after the accident in the Marcasse mine. The man was a habitual drinker, "an unbeliever and a blasphemer," according to the people who told me the story. When Vincent entered his house to help and comfort him, he was received with a volley of abuse. He was called especially a "rosary chewer," as if he had been a Roman Catholic priest. But van Gogh's evangelical tenderness converted the man.[48]

The church sponsoring Vincent's work sent an inspector to report on the young evangelist's progress. The report was scathing, calling Pastor van Gogh's behavior overly zealous, bordering on the scandalous, and his lack of concern for his external appearance unbecoming of a clergyman. While acknowledging his self-sacrifice for "the sick and wounded," the church council concluded van Gogh's lack of "certain qualities may render the exercise of an evangelist's principle function wholly impossible."[49] They withdrew their support after six months.

Vincent attempted to continue his ministry with the poor miners but, lacking financial and material support, it was not to be. His genuine attempt to love people as Christ commanded had been rejected by Christ's own church. Vincent simply didn't conform to external standards of acceptability. The rejection sent him spiraling downward and planted the seeds of his later disdain for the institutional church. Eventually his father came to retrieve him from Belgium, finding his son lying on straw in his tiny hut, physically sick and emaciated, surrounded by the black-faced miners he loved.

Van Gogh's experience as a missionary in Belgium may have been the inspiration behind his painting of the Good Samaritan. *(See color insert, Image 4.)* Although the focus of the composition is clearly the Samaritan lifting the victim onto his horse, in the distance one can make out the two previous travelers who passed by the man without showing compassion. Vincent is contrasting the Samaritan's love with the others' apathy. In Jesus' telling of the story these characters were a priest and a Levite — two devout clergymen. They conformed to every external requirement of religious law. But their godly identities were façades to hide the absence of divine love in their hearts.

The twist in Jesus' story is that the compassionate man is a Samaritan — a label synonymous with ungodliness and heresy to Jewish audiences at the time. Jesus is making the point that external brands don't matter to God, only love. This perspective is echoed by van Gogh when he wrote, "It is good to love many things, for therein lies true strength; whosoever loves much, performs and accomplishes much, and what is done in love is well done."[50]

In his composition the figures of the priest and the Levite are shadowy. Their external religious branding is unimportant. Instead, the viewer's eye, like God's, is drawn immediately to the Samaritan. His crimson turban stands in contrast to every other color in the painting as if to say, *Here is something different; this is what matters.* External conformity, religious apparel, and proper Christian branding are meaningless. Such things will be forgotten in the shadows. "For the LORD sees not as man sees: man looks on the outward appearance, but the LORD looks on the heart."[51]

CHAPTER 4

AT ETERNITY'S GATE

*This is far from theology, simply the fact that the poorest
little wood-cutter or peasant on the heath or miner can
have moments of emotion and inspiration which give
him a feeling of an eternal home to which he is near.*

Vincent van Gogh

FAR FROM ALL THEOLOGY

Van Gogh's work with the coal miners in Belgium left him with a profound admiration for the working class. He believed their existence was as
beautiful as it was brutal, and in their simple faith he recognized a spiritual
depth he'd failed to encounter in the institutional church of his upbring-
ing. The poor did not comprehend deep theology, and they didn't practice
acceptable forms of piety. But they possessed God with a raw authenticity
that was both refreshing and attractive to van Gogh. These sentiments
were captured by Vincent in a charcoal drawing made in 1882.

The drawing shows an old peasant man sitting in a chair beside a fire,
his face buried in his hands. *(See color insert, Image 5.)* Though we don't
know whether his posture is the result of exhaustion, grief, or focused
reflection, we do know that he is praying because van Gogh gave the
drawing the English title, *At Eternity's Gate.* He wrote to his brother Theo
concerning the drawing, "This is far from theology, simply the fact that
the poorest little wood-cutter or peasant on the hearth or miner can have
moments of emotion and inspiration which give him a feeling of an eternal
home to which he is near."[1]

Despite his growing disillusionment with the church, Vincent continued to uphold his belief in God and our ability to commune with him.
He believed the Eternal could be sought not merely within the hallowed

walls of churches and cathedrals, but also sitting at home near a fire. Vincent said, "I think there is no better place for meditation than by a rustic hearth and an old cradle with a baby in it, with a window overlooking a delicate green grainfield and the waving of the alder bushes."[2] God could be encountered outside the clergy-led experiences of the church by ordinary wood-cutters and miners, people who could not grasp theology but still managed to grasp the infinite. The simple act of prayer transported these peasants to the gates of eternity, something the institutional church was failing to do.

VISITING THE ORACLE

The 1999 movie *The Matrix* includes a scene where Neo, the suspected messiah, is taken to visit the Oracle—a mystic with the power to see the future and confirm Neo's destiny. After a nervous drive to the Oracle's apartment, Neo is surprised to discover the clairvoyant is a sweet grandmother who dispenses cryptic wisdom while baking cookies in her kitchen.

I know exactly how Neo felt. As our car arrived outside the modest house I shifted nervously in the back seat. Inside resided my Oracle, a man whose reputation I'd heard about for years. He was an ecclesial clairvoyant (a.k.a. church consultant). My more experienced colleagues at the church had brought me here to discuss our new ministry that was struggling to grow—a ministry I was leading. They hoped the Oracle's wisdom would illuminate the path to success.

I entered the house nervously. The '60s era furniture was covered in plastic, and every horizontal surface was stacked with books. The Oracle looked to be in his seventies, his wrinkled face showing two or three days of stubble growth, and his trousers held to his belly by suspenders. He wore only a tight-fitting undershirt popularly called a "wife-beater." After opening the door he sat in his recliner and never left it. Unfortunately my Oracle didn't bake cookies.

I let my colleagues do the talking. After the pleasantries the Oracle asked to see "our numbers." We handed over the papers. These were records of our church attendance, broken down by worship service, as well as giving trends, and the seating capacity of our building. The Oracle had requested nothing else. My two colleagues and I exchanged eye contact with each other while the old man adjusted his bifocals and repeatedly cleared phlegm from his throat. Without taking his eyes off the papers he finally spoke.

"A few weeks ago I had a leaky pipe in the kitchen. Nasty things, leaky pipes. We used to have a nice little hardware store up the street. It was small, but it was all we had. It's gone now." I looked at my colleagues. *Is this how he always talks?* I asked with my eyes.

The Oracle continued, still studying our numbers. "So, I got in my car and went to the Home Depot. You know the one. It's orange. You can't miss it. Sure enough, Home Depot had the part I needed. They have every part anyone has ever needed." He paused for a moment, and then started up again. "I like to drive," he said.

Oh no, I thought, *he's got dementia, or maybe Alzheimer's. That explains the stubble. He can't remember where his razor is.*

"I drive all over the place."

Yeah, 'cause you're confused.

"And you know what? There are Home Depots everywhere. And they always look the same. Orange. I say to my wife, 'Look! There's another one,' and she laughs at me."

And probably rolls her eyes.

"And when you go inside, they are all the same too. The plumbing aisle is always the plumbing aisle." He chuckled at himself.

Finally, the Oracle put down the papers and looked at us. "You need to become Home Depot," he said lucidly. It was a creepy moment. I felt like Luke Skywalker in Yoda's hut. I wanted to check behind the chair to see if Frank Oz was controlling the old man.

"Every time a person sees your church's name, no matter where it is, they need to know what they're going to get. You need to create an experience and give them that experience every time, in every service, in every location."

My colleague respectfully interrupted. "Yes, but what about the fourth worship service we've just started on Sunday nights? Do you think it will work?" The Oracle looked at the spreadsheets again.

"Yes," he said. "But you need to think about your fifth, sixth, and seventh services. You need to define your *experience* for people and franchise it. That is how you will grow."

"There." The Oracle pointed at me. "In that stack is something for you." He pointed to a book beside the sofa. I was bumbling through the stack. There must have been forty books on the end table. Apparently he believed everyone was clairvoyant. "The black one," he said impatiently. People with recliners that have a permanent imprint of their body shape have no right to be impatient.

I finally found it. "That is the book you must read," he said. "It will help you understand what your church must do." In my hand was *The Experience Economy*, by B. Joseph Pine II and James H. Gilmore. I glanced at the description on the dust jacket: "What would your customers really value? Better yet, for what would they pay a premium? *Experiences*. Make no mistake, say Pine and Gilmore: goods and services are no longer enough. Experiences are the foundation for future economic [and apparently, church] growth."[3]

The Oracle had spoken.

No Experience Necessary

What the Oracle didn't know was that James Gilmore, one of the economists who authored *The Experience Economy*, had recently been interviewed by my other set of colleagues from *Leadership Journal* — Marshall Shelley (MS), Eric Reed (ER), and Kevin Miller (KM). The following is from their conversation which began at the House of Blues Hotel in Chicago.[4]

> **Jim Gilmore:** This was in the nightstand beside my bed. It's their version of the Gideon Bible, a card that says, "Call the front desk to order the religious reading material of your choice." And you can choose from the Bible, the Koran, the writings of Confucius, Buddha, the Dalai Lama, or a book of voodoo spells.
>
> **KM:** So why do you stay here?
>
> **Gilmore:** This hotel is a good example of what's happening in our society. The melting pot of values in America is represented here in the lobby, brought together in a way that creates a sense that one has experienced something unique.
>
> **MS:** The jazz, Gospel, and even African tribal decor we can understand, and the artwork by B. B. King, certainly, but the first thing you see inside the door is Buddha! What's that have to do with the blues?
>
> **Gilmore:** It says we all have the blues. Esthetically, it works. It's Indian and African, New Orleans and Persian, but it's harmonized. Most people who visit won't see a conflict between B. B. King and Buddha. Besides, it's fascinating to have a 2,600-year-old doorman.

ER: Let's head over to Starbucks.

MS: Yes, teach us as we go. The Experience Economy isn't just a Las Vegas phenomenon, is it?

Gilmore: I took pastors on a tour of Las Vegas because I wanted them to understand that everything they see there is coming to their town. And the mindset is entering their churches.

Just look around. There are dozens of clear examples here: FAO Schwarz, ESPN Zone, DisneyQuest. Any town with an upscale coffee shop has a good example of a staged experience. Experiences have become the basis of everyday commerce.

Waiter: What can I get you?

Gilmore: A mocha frappe grande, please.

KM: How does this coffee shop show us that the economy has changed?

Gilmore: Starbucks isn't just about coffee. It's about the coffee-drinking experience.

MS: So how did we arrive at an economy based on buying and selling "experiences"?

Gilmore: Commerce has moved through three economic phases and is now entering a fourth. First was the Agrarian Economy in which economic value was based on the ability to extract commodities—grain, minerals—from the earth. Next came the Industrial Economy built on the ability to make goods from those commodities. Next came the Service Economy: providers perform various services for clients. Now we've entered a new era, the Experience Economy.

Think about a birthday cake. Fifty years ago, mothers made birthday cakes from scratch. A few commodities—flour, butter, sugar, and eggs—cost less than a dollar. Next, as the Industrial Economy advanced, moms used packaged goods (cake mix) and paid a couple of dollars to Betty Crocker for the pre-mixed ingredients. Then came the bakery-made cake, a service many thought well worth the $15 it cost, because time is worth more than money to many people.

Now the homemade birthday cake has been replaced by the birthday experience. Chuck E. Cheese or Jeepers stages a memorable birthday event. You are witnessing the Experience Economy at work.

KM: But home birthday parties always included pin the tail on the donkey. Isn't that an experience?

Gilmore: Yes, we've always had experiences, but we didn't pay someone else to provide them. That's what's changed. We willingly pay to experience things people once did for themselves. At the same time, our expectations about what we get for our money have risen, and with them the lengths to which experience providers must go to satisfy their customers. A place here in Chicago does it as well as anyone: American Girl Place.

KM: Let's go!

Gilmore: We named this the "Experience Stager of the Year" two years ago.

The number one question people ask me when they come here is, "Where's the store?" It doesn't look like a store, and you can't find a gift shop. The whole place is the offering, but they've broken the "store" paradigm.

Inside the front door we have the concierge desk. Here you can buy tickets to the American Girl Revue or make arrangements to eat at the café, which is upstairs with the photo studio and the doll beauty salon. There's also a library and a gallery. Each of the seven dolls is cast in an historic era, has her own nationality or ethnicity, and a whole collection of books and accessories.

KM: This has a museum feel.

Gilmore: Very much. It's not cluttered with merchandise. Everything is showcased.

ER: But all of this is for sale.

Gilmore: Notice the cards. Each pictures a different accessory. You can take the card to the counter and a clerk will bring you the item. Or, you can just collect the cards—part memorabilia, part aspiration.

KM: A wish list. Give this to Grandma so she'll know what to get you.

Gilmore: A work associate of mine brought his two nieces here and spent $400. Lunch is $16 per person. You can have your doll's hair styled, get your photo on the cover of an *American Girl* magazine, go to the theater. For a group of four, you could easily spend a couple hundred dollars before you've bought a single physical thing. People are buying experiences.

MS: So how does all this "experience providing" apply to the church?

Gilmore: It doesn't. When the church gets into the business of staging experiences, that quickly becomes idolatry.

MS: I'm stunned. So you don't encourage churches to use your elements of marketable experiences to create attractive experiences for their attenders?

Gilmore: No. The organized church should never try to stage a God experience.

KM: When people come to church, don't they expect an experience of some kind? Consumers approach the worship service with the same mindset as they do a purchase.

Gilmore: Increasingly you find people talking about the worship *experience* rather than the worship *service*. That reflects what's happening in the outside world. I'm dismayed to see churches abandon the means of grace that God ordains simply to conform to the patterns of the world.

KM: So what happens in church? Are people getting a service, because they're helped to do something they couldn't do on their own, that is, get closer to God? Or are they getting an experience, the encounter with God through worship?

Gilmore: The word "getting" is, I think, the problem with contemporary Christianity. God is the audience of worship. What you get is, quite frankly, irrelevant as a starting point.

ER: But people, especially unchurched people, don't perceive it that way. They're expecting some return.

Gilmore: They may come that way at first: "Give me, feed me, make me feel good." But they should be led to say, "Hey, this is not about *me*, God. Worship is to glorify *you*."

KM: But if my mission is to reach a consumerist culture — if I'm going to get a hearing for my message — then I'm going to have to provide something that the consumer considers of value.

Gilmore: That is the argument. But the only thing of value the church has to offer is the gospel. I believe that one result of the emerging Experience Economy will be a longing for *authenticity*. To the extent that the church stages worldly experiences, it will lose its effectiveness.

ER: So people simply need an authentic experience of God.

Gilmore: I once had a Catholic friend visit me for the weekend. On Sunday, I asked if he wanted to go to church with me. It was a new church, just starting. We were meeting in a gym with folding chairs.

He agreed to go, and frankly, I was kind of embarrassed. You know — the gym, the clanky piano, certainly no impressive music or drama.

Afterward I said, "Sam, I apologize for the service today."

"Apologize?" he said. "No. It was wonderful."

I was stunned. "How so?"

"The fact that all of you wanted to be gathered for that spoke to me."

MS: What comes *after* the Experience Economy? Will people ever tire of seeking new sensations?

Gilmore: After a while, thoughtful people begin to ask, "What effect are all these experiences having on me? What am I becoming?" That's why we think that the Experience Economy will eventually give way to the Transformation Economy. But in the church, it's God who's doing the transforming.

But, look, I'm not a pastor; I'm an economist. Pastors may see applications from our book that we didn't intend. But I don't want pastors to use our book as a manual for changing their churches.

MS: Well, thanks for the tour. We're headed to the ESPN Zone for lunch.

Gilmore: Great place. Restaurant, sports entertainment, art gallery, and gaming arcade all rolled into one. Certainly a great experience.

COME ONE, COME ALL

Something is wrong when an economist recognizes the dangers of staging experiences in church and a church consultant does not. It reveals the power consumerism has attained over the Christian imagination. We assume, without pausing for critical reflection, that the church's mission will be advanced by creating external spiritual experiences for people. Most often these take the form of a Sunday worship service.

One pastor advocating this experienced-based approach describes his church's emphasis this way:

> It is our desire not to merely have a church service, but to create an experience through song, video, messages, and any other tools the Holy Spirit might place in front of us.... I believe a boring church is a sin! So, we are going to always do all we can to make sure that when a person attends our church on Sunday that it is one of the best hours of their week. I believe people should look forward more to church than *24*, *Lost*, or *American Idol*.[5]

Though few pastors would say their church is attempting to be more entertaining than network television, the motivation behind his emphasis on experience is quite common. He believes orchestrated experiences are used by God to transform lives. He continues, "I have told people not to miss one single Sunday in December because our team has put together some stuff that we know God is going to use to impact thousands of lives."[6]

Pastors Tim Stevens and Tony Morgan encourage church leaders to "embrace entertainment" in their book, *Simply Strategic Growth: Attracting a Crowd to Your Church*. And like many others, their motivation is life transformation. They write, "We are about entertainment to the extent that it allows us to captivate the minds and hearts of those who don't yet know Jesus."[7] To that end, Stevens and Morgan insist that staging an upbeat worship service is the key. To infuse the proper level of energy they recommend "pumping up the volume ... louder music creates more energy."[8] Tempo is also important. "Songs that are upbeat and more celebratory in nature will generate a positive response from the congregation."[9] They also advise people on the platform to "practice looking happy" and "make sure you're strategically using humor."[10] As the title of their book reveals, the reason for micromanaging the staged worship experience is to attract a crowd.

These pastors, representative of so many contemporary Christians, believe that God changes lives through the commodification and consumption of experiences. If our worship gatherings are energetic, stimulating, and exciting enough then people will attend, receive what's being communicated, and be spiritually transformed. The justification for this approach is simple — people won't come to a church that's boring. And what qualifies as boring is defined by our consumer/experience economy. But the moment we believe transformation occurs via external experiences, the emphasis of the ministry must adjust accordingly. Manufacturing experiences and meticulously controlling staged environments become the means for advancing Christ's mission. And the role of the pastor, once imagined as a shepherd tending a flock, now conjures images of a circus ringmaster shouting, "Come one, come all, to the greatest show on earth!" In Consumer Christianity, the shepherd becomes a showman.

To be fair, there is nothing new about entertainment-driven worship. American Christianity, going back to the nineteenth-century revivals of Charles Finney, has employed staged experiences as a tool of spiritual transformation. Jeanne Halgren Kilde traces this phenomenon in her book, *When Church Became Theater*. In the early 1800s, worship was dominated by preaching with a limited amount of hymn singing, but by mid-century

Americans were becoming enamored with European "art-music." The desire to hear professionally performed music soon entered the church and battle lines were drawn. Those in favor of congregational hymn singing argued that "worship by proxy" was no worship at all. Others recognized that attracting a crowd to church would require accommodating popular expectations. In other words, using entertainment.

By the late nineteenth century the debate was over. In 1875, Josiah Holland wrote, "The churches are full, as a rule, where the music is excellent. This fact may not be very flattering to preachers, but it is a fact."[11] While hymn singing did not disappear, worship quickly adopted the values of a professional performance with an increasingly passive audience. During this same period the architecture of America's church changed considerably. Gone were the old Puritan meetinghouses. Massive organs and choir lofts became commonplace, as did auditorium-style seating and stage lighting. A new building form emerged—a hybrid that was part cathedral and part theater. What I call "catheaters" are still popular in church design today, although of a sort fitting our digital age.

Decades earlier many clergy had condemned theaters as places of sensuality and debauchery, but by the late 1800s they readily hired theater architects to design their churches. It was a case of form following function. Like theaters, churches had become places where the middle class gathered to be entertained by gifted orators and professional musicians. "Driven by the power of the marketplace, rather than tradition, secular auditoriums were more responsive to consumers'—that is, audiences'—needs."[12] Hoping to attract the same middle-class consumers, churches quickly adopted the designs of secular auditoriums. In a self-reinforcing cycle, churches adopting theater architecture found their worship becoming more like entertainment which, in turn, necessitated more theatrical church buildings.

The emergence of suburban megachurches in the late twentieth century is the product of this century-old cycle. As Kilde notes, megachurches "carry on the strategies that evangelical churches adopted in the 1870s and 1880s."[13] And, "while contemporary church leaders might speak much more freely about the need to entertain their audiences than did their late nineteenth-century counterparts, their goals remain quite similar."[14]

Before we assume the production of spiritual experiences is merely a Christian trend, we should remember that consumerism does not discriminate. One hundred and fifty years after the American church adopted these values, we are now seeing non-Western religions adopt them as well. In 2006, the Swaminarayan Akshardham temple near Dehli, India, opened to the public. Along with the traditional Hindu architectural elements there is also an indoor boat ride, movie theater, musical fountain, and a hall of animatronic figures. The temple's designers found their inspiration by visiting America's most popular tourist destination—Walt Disney World. Like Consumer Christianity, Consumer Hinduism is blurring the line between worship and amusement with the hope of attracting a crowd.

COMING DOWN THE MOUNTAIN

In 1515, Michelangelo completed a sculpture of Moses. The marble figure depicts an old, but very muscular, Moses seated with the Ten Commandments under his arm and a billowing beard. Tourists are often shocked to see what appear to be horns protruding from Moses' head. The figure looks more like the devil than Israel's deliverer.

The presence of horns on Michelangelo's Moses can be traced to a mistranslation of the Bible in the fifth century. The story from Exodus 34 says that after meeting with the Lord on Mount Sinai, Moses came down the mountain with the Ten Commandments. When the people saw him they were afraid because "the skin of his face shone."[15] Standing in God's glory had somehow transfigured Moses' appearance. His face was literally radiant. The Hebrew word refers to a *beam* or *ray of light*. But when St. Jerome converted the ancient Scriptures into Latin, he mistranslated the word as "horns." So, when Michelangelo read his Bible he believed the people were frightened by Moses' appearance because he had grown horns while meeting with God on the mountain.

St. Jerome's Latin translation of the Bible, the Vulgate, had been used for nearly a thousand years before Michelangelo put chisel to stone. The erroneously-horned Moses reminds us that questioning popular assumptions is important. But unfortunately, Moses' experience with God on the mountain is still widely misunderstood, and largely unquestioned, today. We no longer foolishly depict Moses with horns, but our misunderstanding of his mountaintop experience is still embarrassingly displayed virtually every Sunday.

In Exodus 34 we are told that Moses covered his face with a veil so that the people would not be frightened by his appearance. But according to the apostle Paul in the New Testament, Moses covered himself with a veil so the people couldn't see that the glory was fading away.[16] Whatever transformation Moses experienced in God's presence on the mountain was temporary, and the veil hid the transient nature of this glory from the people. His mountaintop experience was genuine, glorious, and full of God's presence—but it did not bring lasting transformation. This is the critical part of the story we seem to have forgotten.

Moses' experience is all too common among Christians today. Through the influence of our consumer culture, we've come to believe that transformation is attained through external experiences. And, as we've already seen, many churches have engineered their ministries to manufacture these experiences for crowds of religious consumers. We've come to regard our church buildings, with their multimedia theatrical equipment, as mountaintops where God's glory resides and may be encountered by mere mortals. One pastor, explaining why his church opened another location across town, said "We decided, if you can't get the people to the mountain, bring the mountain to the people."[17]

Ascending the mountain every Sunday morning, millions of Christians want to have an experience with God, and this is precisely what churches promise. And not disappointed, many leave these experiences with a sense of transformation or inspiration. They feel "pumped up," "fed," or "on fire for the Lord." No doubt many people, like Moses, have authentic experiences of God through these events. Others may simply be carried along by the music, crowd, and energy of the room. Whether a result of God or group, what is beyond question is that many people depart feeling spiritually rejuvenated and capable of taking on life for another six days.

The problem with these external experiences, as Moses discovered, is that the transformation doesn't last. In a few days time, or maybe as early as Sunday lunch, the glory begins to fade. The mountaintop experience with God—the event you were certain would change your life forever—turns out to be another fleeting spiritual high. And to hide the lack of genuine transformation, we mask the inglorious truth of our lives behind a veil, a façade of Christian piety, until we can ascend the mountain again and be recharged.

This philosophy of spiritual formation through the consumption of external experiences creates worship junkies—Christians who leap from one mountaintop to another, one spiritual high to another, in search of a glory that does not fade. In response, churches and Christian conferences are driven to create ever-grander experiences and more elaborate productions to satisfy expectations. Ironically, these worship spectacles, according to Sally Morgenthaler, are failing to produce real worshipers. She writes:

> We are not producing worshippers in this country. Rather we are producing a generation of spectators, religious onlookers lacking, in many cases, any memory of a true encounter with God, deprived of both the tangible sense of God's presence and the supernatural relationship their inmost spirits crave.[18]

Ministries that focus on manufacturing spiritual experiences, despite their laudable intentions, may actually be retarding spiritual growth by making people experience-dependent. Like caged animals, Consumer Christians lose the ability to do what they were designed by God to do—have a vibrant, self-generating relationship with Christ. Instead, they become dependent upon their zookeeper-pastors for life and nourishment. This captive/captor relationship is unlikely to change as long as both the church member and leader are satisfied with the arrangement. But is this what the Christian life is supposed to be? What about the tangible sense of God's presence we crave in our inmost spirits that Morgenthaler writes about?

In the New Testament, Jesus and his apostles do not emphasize external experiences as the means of encountering God. Instead, their focus is upon a mysterious communion with God made possible through the indwelling presence of his Holy Spirit. Contrasting the fading glory that Moses experienced on Sinai, the apostle Paul says that we are being transformed "from one degree of glory to another," and that this comes from the Spirit.[19] This transformation is not from the outside working in, but from the inside working out. What Jesus spoke of in John 4 has come to pass. We no longer worship the Father on a mountain or in Jerusalem, but in spirit and truth.[20] To encounter the glory of God no longer requires ascending a mountain, but learning to embrace a divine mystery—"Christ *in* you, the hope of glory."[21]

When we expect transformation to occur through external experiences, we are opting for an inferior model of spiritual formation. As a result, many Consumer Churches have inadvertently dismissed the new covenant in Christ and returned to the shadows of the old covenant by building temples and climbing mountains to catch glimpses of a fading glory. The reason for this regression is simple—New Testament spirituality, properly understood, is immune to the forces of consumerism. An internal communion with God through the Spirit cannot be packaged, commodified, and marketed to religious consumers. It cannot be bundled, branded, or put on display to draw a crowd.

A word of caution: Worship gatherings are not necessarily the problem. The early Christians gathered regularly for worship, and the writer of Hebrews even commands his readers to not neglect meeting together as some were in the habit of doing (10:25). The problem is not our gatherings, but what we expect from them. If corporate worship is an external display of an internal reality—the glory of Christ that abides within—then these gatherings will not be full of passive spectators. These events will be where Christians gather to show a watching world the continual worship that marks their lives—whether it is celebratory, reflective, or even repentant.

However, if people have no sustainable communion with Christ through his indwelling Spirit, they will come to worship seeking a temporary filling, a transient dose of glory to carry them along. And rather than reflecting the full spectrum of the human-divine relationship as revealed in Scripture, particularly the Psalms, these gatherings will fixate on only one element—the celebratory. Over time, as the familiar experience offers a diminishing return, religious consumers will either demand more energy through innovation, or they will shift to another church looking for a new experience. They will be drawn by promises of transformation and a genuine encounter with God, but will they leave these experiences radiating the unfading glory of the Lord, or merely sprouting the horns of consumerism?

O BROTHER, WHERE ART THOU?

The alternative to prefabricated-experience spirituality is what has been practiced by Christians for centuries: prayer. I'm not speaking of prayer in the sense that many people understand the term today, but rather a profoundly intimate, internal, and spiritual communion with God, the kind practiced by a seventeenth-century monk known as Brother Lawrence. His grasp of New Testament spirituality, the glory accessible through the indwelling Spirit, has made Brother Lawrence admired by Catholics and Protestants alike. John Wesley and more recently A.W. Tozer both recommended reading Brother Lawrence's collection of reflections and conversations, *The Practice of the Presence of God*.

IMAGE 1: Vincent van Gogh, *Starry Night*
1889, oil on canvas

IMAGE 2: Ron English, *Starry Night Urban Sprawl*
2003, oil on canvas
Reprinted with permission

IMAGE 3: Vincent van Gogh, *The Raising of Lazarus*
1890, oil on canvas

IMAGE 5: Vincent van Gogh, *At Eternity's Gate*
1882, lithograph

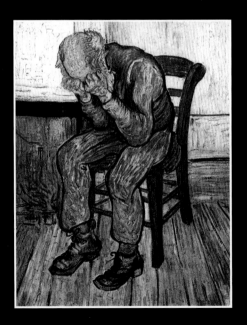

IMAGE 6: Vincent van Gogh, *At Eternity's Gate*
1890, oil on canvas

IMAGE 7: Vincent van Gogh, *Augustine Roulin "La Berceuse"*
1888, oil on canvas

IMAGE 8: Vincent van Gogh, *Still Life with Open Bible*
1885, oil on canvas

IMAGE 9: Vincent van Gogh, *Olive Trees*
1889, oil on canvas

IMAGE 10: Vincent van Gogh, *The Yellow House*
1888, oil on canvas

IMAGE 11: Vincent van Gogh, *The Potato Eaters*
1885, oil on canvas

IMAGE 12: Vincent van Gogh, *The Sower*
1888, oil on canvas

Brother Lawrence was born Nicholas Herman in eastern France. A life of poverty led him to enlist in the army for a meager salary and regular meals. In the winter of his eighteenth year he was converted to Christ by a tree. In truth, the barren tree was used by God to trigger a revelation in the young soldier's imagination. Nicholas said that through the tree "he received a high view of the providence and power of God ... and it kindled in him such a love for God" that it never faded from his soul. Six years later he entered a monastery and took the name "Lawrence of the Resurrection."

For the remainder of his life, Brother Lawrence worked in a kitchen, and it was among the pots and pans that he would experienced a sweet communion with God. He believed firmly that all of life was sacred, and those who believed times of corporate worship drew one closer to God suffered from "a great delusion." With words that are still relevant today, Lawrence said, "Men invent means and methods of coming at God's love, they learn rules and set up devices to remind them of that love, and it seems like a world of trouble to bring oneself into the consciousness of God's presence. Yet it might be so simple. Is it not quicker and easier just to do our common business wholly for the love of him?"[22]

Rather than seeking external experiences to fuel his spirituality, Brother Lawrence cultivated a life of ceaseless prayer as the apostle Paul advised.[23] With a sanctified imagination, he engaged his "common business" feverishly in the kitchen ever mindful of God's presence. He recalls, "As often as I could, I placed myself as a worshiper before him, fixing my mind upon his holy presence, recalling it when I found it wandering from him. This proved to be an exercise frequently painful, yet I persisted through all difficulties." Ever radiating the joy and peace of Christ, Lawrence attracted others to his simple practice. "There is not in the world a kind of life more sweet and delightful, than that of a continual conversation with God; those only can comprehend it who practice and experience it."[24]

The use of the imagination in prayer was not originated by Brother Lawrence. Many others throughout church history have advocated a similar means of communing with God. Origen, Gregory of Nyssa, Julian of Norwich, Francis de Sales, and, most notably, Ignatius of Loyola are just a few. Ignatius taught Christians to inhabit biblical stories with their imaginations, using all five senses to place themselves into scenes with Jesus. As odd as this practice might sound to contemporary evangelicals, there is evidence that such practices may have been intended by the biblical writers themselves. After all, how can one read about Jesus as the Good Shepherd without imagining a shepherd? Such vivid language is intended to prick the imagination.

Even more intriguing is a concession made by the translators of the New American Standard Bible. In a foreword to the Bible titled "Notes on the Translation of the Greek Tenses" they write:

> In regard to the use of the historic present, the Board recognized that in some contexts the present tense seems more unexpected and unjustified to the English reader than the past tense would have been. But *Greek authors frequently used the present tense for the sake of heightened vividness, thereby transporting their readers in imagination to the actual scene at the time of occurrence.* However the Board felt that it would be wise to change these historic presents into English past tenses.[25] [emphasis added]

The gospel writers may have used this Greek literary device because it fit their own Hebrew worldview. "To a Hebrew, to remember meant to re-experience in the present the power and effect of a past event."[26] Remembrance was not merely an act of recollection, but an act of reliving. For the Hebrew mind this required more than logical faculties; it required the imagination. Consistent with this understanding, one pastor notes, "Information alone never leads to transformation. Rather, it is what we experience as real on the inside that transforms us. That is all about the use of the imagination."[27]

Unfortunately, this ancient practice of imaginative prayer is all too rare among contemporary Christians. There may be at least two reasons. First, prayer in general isn't a high value in most churches. George Barna reports that prayer is listed among top priorities by less than one in twenty-five churches.[28] Although rhetoric about having "a personal relationship with God" is pervasive, actually teaching and modeling such communion with God is woefully absent in the contemporary church. Far more energy is poured into the Sunday morning experience than actually equipping people to internally experience God throughout their "common business."

The other reason imaginative prayer is a foreign concept today may be our diminished ability to imagine at all. Our image-saturated culture means that the imagination isn't required the way it once was. TV, film, and video game producers have done the imaginative work for us. Instead, we ingest ready-made images like junk food—they satisfy our desires temporarily, but ultimately diminish the strength of our minds. The commonsense wisdom of "use it or lose it" describes our condition well. Rick Richardson, an Anglican priest, evangelist, and proponent of imaginative prayer, says:

> We have immense difficulty practicing God's presence and keeping God's reality before our mind's eye because we have dismissed or denigrated our capacity to intuitively and imaginatively apprehend and encounter God. We have lost the power of imagination and intuition.[29]

Reigniting the ancient practice of imaginative prayer isn't going to occur through multimillion-dollar catheaters and digital worship extravaganzas. These drive-through encounters with God are impressive, but by rewarding passivity they may actually contribute to the atrophy of our imaginations. They cannot train us in the sweet and delightful life of ceaseless prayer which requires effort and intuition. For that we need mentors—living and dead—men and women like Brother Lawrence, Teresa of Avila, Thomas Kelly, Evelyn Underhill, and their contemporary counterparts to guide us. Personal mentoring in prayer is necessary because, as Brother Lawrence said, "those only can comprehend it who practice and experience it."

LIGHT UNCREATED

Eight years after creating his charcoal sketch of the old man deep in prayer, van Gogh recreated the composition with oil paints. *(See color insert, Image 6.)* Exactly why Vincent chose to remake this image from the thousands of drawings he'd sketched is a mystery, but his circumstances at the time may give some clues.

In 1890, Vincent was a patient at the asylum in Saint-Rémy. Perhaps in his agonizing battle with mental illness, he could identify with the old man in prayer—his face buried in his hands seeking God's presence. In his pain, Vincent longed to experience God intimately. He too wanted to reach the gate of eternity and transcend his immediate condition.

The unusual element in the oil version of *At Eternity's Gate* is the man's clothing. Unlike the black-and-white drawing in which Vincent differentiated the man's clothing with shades of gray, in the oil painting his shirt, pants, and even socks are the same color—blue. We know he used this color in his works to symbolize the infinite. This peasant man, alone on a chair in a barren room, has entered the presence of the Infinite One through prayer.

Vincent's exceptionally high view of prayer began early in his spiritual journey. When still in his father's home, Vincent was influenced by the writings of Friedrich Schleiermacher. Many of Schleiermacher's ideas departed from orthodoxy, but not his belief that religious institutions and orchestrated worship constituted a merely outward manifestation of religion. The true substance of spirituality, he argued, was internal and infinite. Strict adherence to external forms, van Gogh believed, could even be detrimental, obscuring one's encounter with the eternal. Prayer, therefore, was a more essential avenue for communion with God than the institutional experiences of the church.

Later, Vincent found Thomas à Kempis' classic work, *Imitation of Christ*, to be a spiritual resource second only to the Bible. He read the book repeatedly throughout his life. In it Kempis contrasts the surpassing greatness of communing directly with God versus all other intermediaries. "But the difference is great—yes, very great, indeed—between delight in the Creator and in the creature, in eternity and in time, in Light uncreated and in the light that is reflected."[30]

After his disillusionment with the institutional church following his missionary service, van Gogh came to see whatever glory existed in the church as reflected light. But in most cases, as his paintings reveal, he saw no light in the institutional church at all. The efforts of institutions to reflect God's glory and disperse it to the masses were flawed. They diminished the beauty and power that was the essence of true religion. Instead, van Gogh celebrated the "Light uncreated" that he believed was accessible to all through prayer. Our longing to pass through the gates of eternity will not be satisfied by any external experience, but by the dwelling of God within. Relying on external experiences will only offer glimpses of a reflected glory, and the resulting joy will be fleeting. Instead, our longing should be no different than that of Thomas à Kempis:

> O Light eternal, surpassing all created brightness, flash forth the lightning from above and enlighten the inmost recesses of my heart. Cleanse, cheer, enlighten, and enliven my spirit with all its powers, that it may cling to you in ecstasies of joy. Oh, when will that happy and wished-for hour come, when you will fill me with your presence and become all in all to me? So long as this is not given me, my joy will not be complete.[31]

CHAPTER 5

WIND IN A BOTTLE

I prefer painting people's eyes to cathedrals. For there
is something in the eyes that is not in the cathedral,
however solemn and imposing the latter may be—
a human soul, be it that of a poor beggar or of
a street walker, is more interesting to me.

Vincent van Gogh

FROM CROSSING TO CRUISING

Throughout the first half of the twentieth century, New York Harbor
bustled with ocean liners transporting thousands of people between North
America and Europe every week. Great ships like the *Queen Mary* and
Normandie were celebrated as floating palaces, but they served a highly
utilitarian purpose—moving passengers and cargo from point A to point
B, hence the name "liners." These ships were the lifeline between the old
world and the new. They were so vital that the North Atlantic became a
key theater of battle in both world wars.

Despite New York's congested harbor, competition between shipping lines
was a secondary consideration. Most liners were operated by governments as
ships of state, and choices were limited. Sailing to England? Cunard/White
Star was your line. Amsterdam? You'd be departing from the Holland-America
Line pier in Hoboken. Want to visit Paris in the springtime? You'd sail the
French Line. In addition, the demand for passage between Europe and North
America was so strong that shipping lines did not need to compete. The only
real rivalry was over the Blue Riband—the prize given to the ship able to
cross the North Atlantic fastest. But this was more a matter of national pride
than commercial competition. The last liner to be awarded the trophy was
the *S.S. United States* in 1952, but the victory was to be short lived.

The following year a Comet roared above the Atlantic. The De Havilland Comet was the first commercial jetliner. In six hours it traveled the distance covered by the *S.S. United States* in six days, and virtually overnight the immense Atlantic Ocean became "the pond." As air travel became more affordable, shipping lines found themselves competing for a rapidly shrinking number of passengers. Government funding was revoked, and ships were laid up. (The *United States* has been rusting at a pier in Philadelphia since 1969.) The golden age of the ocean liners was over, and many predicted passenger shipping would never recover.

But a handful of inventive ship owners concocted a new way for their mothballed fleets to produce revenue: cruises. Abandoning the practical function of transporting people from point A to point B, cruises sailed in a circuit, embarking and disembarking passengers from the same port. Unlike the liners' utilitarian purpose, cruises were designed for leisure. Some old liners that had been headed to the scrappers were refurbished and redeployed to warmer latitudes. The decks once crowded with impoverished immigrants straining to see the Statue of Liberty were now filled with pensioned tourists straining for a banana daiquiri.

The new focus on leisure meant the ship was no longer strictly a means of transportation; it had become the destination. Unlike the old Atlantic shipping lines, cruise operators had no incentive to move passengers off their ships at each port-of-call because passengers who stayed aboard would also spend their money aboard. Increasing the number of entertainment options on the ship became their goal. This triggered a rapid increase in the size of vessels built by the cruise lines, each one incorporating more of the features vacationers wanted. As a result, many of today's gargantuan cruise ships dwarf the ocean liners of the past—something no one would have predicted forty years ago when passenger shipping was believed to be on its deathbed.

In May 2005, the largest passenger ship ever built sailed into New York Harbor where the *Queen Mary* and *Normandie* once reigned. At twice their size, Royal Caribbean's *Freedom of the Seas* boasts five swimming pools, a rock-climbing wall, miniature golf course, multiple theaters and restaurants, and even an ice skating rink. The cruise line's chairman said the ship's name was chosen "deliberately to convey the enormity of features and amenities offered on this extraordinary ship. *Freedom of the Seas* is really all about freedom of choice. Freedom to explore. Freedom to relax. Freedom to make one's own vacation plans reflective of one's own tastes and interests."[1] Although *Freedom of the Seas* will stop at a few Caribbean islands on each cruise, one travel writer notes that "you could never get off the ship and still have the best vacation of your life." And that, according to the cruise lines, is precisely the point.

THE MEGACHURCH SETS SAIL

There was a time when competition among churches was minimal. Although every town had multiple churches and some "sheep swapping" did occur, most people stayed committed to their own congregation. Church attendance was a widely accepted and even prescribed activity for many Americans, so there were plenty of people to fill the pews. The thought of switching congregations was a rare, even bizarre, notion. What would be the purpose of changing churches anyway? Apart from their different theological tacks, they all provided the same utilitarian function of gathering a community and connecting them with God. They spiritually transported people from point A to point B.

American church observer Lyle Schaller comments about this period of noncompetition among churches: "The 1920–70 era represented the peak of an era in American Protestantism that was marked by such concepts and practices as ecumenism, interdenominational cooperation, denominational mergers, comity, and Christian unity."[2] Demand for church was high and competition between churches was considered unnecessary and even unbecoming.

But around the time jetliners began to take over the transatlantic trade from ocean liners, another revolution took hold in the church. The Baby Boomer generation reached adulthood and stopping going to church. Popular culture had undergone a dramatic shift toward secularism, and for the Boomer generation churchgoing was no longer an expectation. The high demand for traditional religion that mainline churches had enjoyed for centuries suddenly dried up. In Europe the post-Christian age was particularly devastating as church attendance plummeted and never recovered. Like the grand ocean liners, many of the oldest and most beautiful churches in the Western world languished away.

The story in North America was different. Traditional churches did struggle, but a new breed of Christian leaders began tinkering to see if rejuvenation was possible. In 1975, a young pastor named Bill Hybels began to wonder why so many of his contemporaries still professed faith but avoided going to church. With members of his youth group, the twenty-three-year-old Hybels began to knock on doors to survey residents in the Chicago area. They asked, "Do you actively attend a local church?" If the answer was no, they followed up with "Why not?" and recorded the reasons. What Hybels discovered was that churches must now compete in a culture of television, rock and roll, and in-your-face entertainment. The old utilitarian function of the church—gathering people and connecting them with God—simply wasn't going to cut it anymore. Americans wanted church to be comfortable, entertaining, relevant, and nonthreatening.

The outcome of the research was the founding of Willow Creek Community Church—arguably the most influential church in America over the last thirty years and prototype of the modern megachurch. Following the feedback from their market research, Willow Creek grew from 125 to 2,000 members in just two years. Today the church welcomes over 20,000 people every week. Hybels, along with other up-and-coming pastors, had shown that people would still attend church in a post-Christian culture if it appealed to their perceived needs and desires.

Whether intentional or accidental, by beginning with the desires of the religious marketplace these pragmatic leaders were redefining the church's purpose. Rather than viewing the church as a *means* to an end (connecting people with God), the church became an end in itself. The logic was simple: If the masses did not feel the need to connect with God then perhaps another "felt need" could draw them into the church. And while they engaged the upbeat music, support groups, dramas, and practical messages, they might just find God too. Of course these innovative pastors, sometimes called "pastorpreneurs," genuinely wanted people to connect with God. That is what motivated them to tinker with the church's failing strategy in the first place. But by starting with consumers' desires, they were mirroring the shift in passenger shipping away from liner voyages to cruising. They were making the church itself the destination rather than the vehicle. New jargon was even developed that captured this shift. While missionary endeavors traditionally sought to reach "non-Christians," the new approach sought to attract the "unchurched."

Repositioning the church to be both the vehicle and the destination triggered explosive growth in the size of congregations. Logic dictated that in a competitive religious marketplace larger churches, like larger cruise ships, could offer consumers more choices. As a result, church growth went from a by-product of the mission to its core. Size became success.

In 1970 there were just ten megachurches in the United States (defined as congregations with weekly attendance above 2,000 people). In 1980 the number had increased to fifty. Ten years later it was 250. And in 2005 there were over 1,200 megachurches. Today, half of all churchgoers in the United States attend the largest 10 percent of churches. What often goes unnoticed, however, are the fifty smaller churches that close their doors every week. As Lyle Schaller writes:

> The veteran leaders of these two congregations keep asking, "Why do the people moving out here prefer one of those megachurches over our congregation?" The most frequent realistic response sounds rude but can be summarized in five words, "Your congregation is not competitive."[3]

And how could it be? Traditional churches were designed for a utilitarian purpose. Moving religious people from point A to point B required minimal accoutrements. The church-as-destination model, however, is constantly incorporating new features to attract more religious consumers. Congregations that fail to recognize this shift are left high and dry. Again, Schaller states it plainly: "The old rule book called for congregations in rural America to cooperate with one another in order to survive. The new rule book calls for congregations in rural America to expand their service area in order to compete for future constituents."[4]

Competition has driven churches to add features, or "service areas," beyond what anyone might have imagined just a few decades ago. Along with the multimedia auditoriums, today's thriving churches also include coffee shops, bookstores, food courts, auto repair shops, day care centers, weight rooms, and themed children's facilities complete with Nintendos and talking animals. James Twitchell compares these churches to medieval fortresses. People may venture outside from time to time, but everything they need is within the walls of the institution. These megachurches are self-contained cities where the faithful can worship, eat, shop, work, and play. One could conceivably never leave and still experience all that the Christian life has to offer. And that is precisely the point.

It's far easier to point out the speck in the megachurch's eye than the plank in our own. In fairness, the cultural forces that have given rise to megachurches are at work in most smaller congregations as well. Even the new crop of emerging churches, alternative churches, and house churches may be the product of consumerism. They can brand themselves as the un-megachurch in the same way that 7-Up is the un-cola, but they are still trying to appeal to market desires—albeit a different market. And they are just as likely to view the church institution, whether large or small, as both the means and end of the mission. Therefore, the maintenance, expansion, and empowerment of the institution are of paramount concern for virtually all churches. We have all swallowed the cultural punch that believes institutions are both the means and the end of God's mission in the world.

"I LOVE WHAT YOU DO FOR ME, TOYOTA!"

In our consumer culture, there is no question the dominant institution is the corporation. Originally, corporations were created by special government charters to protect the state from risk and serve the public interest. They were chartered to build a bridge, extract a natural resource, or transport supplies between colonies. And when the task was accomplished, the state could dissolve the corporation; it was a means to an end. As a result, 150 years ago corporations were not institutions with significant cultural influence. But that changed after the American Civil War.

The Fourteenth Amendment was drafted to guarantee equal rights for the newly emancipated slaves, but business lawyers read an opportunity between the lines. With the Fourteenth Amendment in hand, they argued that a corporation was also a person deserving equal rights under the law. The courts agreed.[5] Ironically, the same law that ensured human beings would no longer have the legal status of property was used to grant property the legal status of human beings. Corporations were now permitted to buy and sell land, sign contracts, and engage governmental systems as independent entities. This meant liability was no longer carried by business owners, managers, or shareholders, but the "person" of the corporation. By the dawn of the twentieth century, businesses that had previously been partnerships or sole proprietorships saw the benefit of reorganizing under the new law.

During this same period the advertising industry came of age to distinguish one corporation from another. As Benjamin Barber points out, "Salt was salt was salt, what was the point of having two or three salt companies?"[6] Branding (as discussed in chapter three) was the psychological device used to lure shoppers to buy one corporation's product rather than the identical item from a competitor. Why buy a faceless commodity when you could buy oats from a smiling Quaker man, or syrup from Aunt Jemima? Through branding corporations came to possess names, faces, and even personalities. They became people in the public's imagination just as they had gained personhood in the courts. Advertising has formed us to give our affection not only to the products we consume, but also to the personified corporations that supply them. We can shout, "I love what you do for me, Toyota!" as if the carmaker was a benevolent individual and not 300,000 anonymous employees organized into a profit-driven multinational institution.

One hundred years of relating to personified corporations has caused a profound shift in the way we live. There was a time when navigating through life meant managing relationships with real people—the tailor, the doctor, the grocer, the minister. They had names, faces, and personalities. You liked some and tolerated others. And through this network you acquired your daily bread. Today, we still depend on a network for survival, but it is increasingly populated with corporations—disembodied persons with names, faces, and personalities imprinted through branding on our imaginations. Old Navy is our tailor, Blue Cross our doctor, Costco our grocer, and our minister? He is now a set of programs bundled together and organized into an institution we nostalgically call "the church."

Enter most church facilities on Sunday and you'll be greeted by a wall display of brochures outlining their programs. The display functions as a menu that religious customers may peruse to satisfy their hunger. If you have a spiritual need, the church institution probably has a program to address it. And if not, a larger church down the road certainly will. Throughout most of history Christian faith has been transmitted life to life. Disciple to disciple. But we no longer expect this to be the case. We can avoid the messy reality of human relationships because somewhere a curriculum has been published, a book has been written, a program has been created to meet our spiritual needs. Who needs a spiritual mother or father? We now have the institution to shepherd us in the faith.

Not far from the brochure wall, if you attend a larger church, you'll probably discover a store selling sermon CDs and Christian books, as well as merchandise branded with the church's logo—Bible covers, golf shirts, hats, mugs, and bumper stickers ("My family and my tithe go to Faith Community Church"). Purchasing and displaying these logo items is a way for the religious consumer to reinforce their relationship with the institution. Through branding a church differentiates itself from all the others offering the same basic product—God. After all, in a competitive religious market the goal is not simply for believers to be dedicated to God, but to the particular institution who supplies him. (Starbucks doesn't want you to buy coffee, they want you to buy *their* coffee.) By giving the institution a face (logo) and personality (brand), it ceases to be an abstract organization, and it becomes a person in our imaginations. Suddenly, we feel affection for Faith Community Church and not just the human beings we know there. We have a relationship with the personified institution that promises to spiritually nurture and feed us. As such, with all sincerity we can say, "I love what you do for me, Faith Community!"

The personification of institutions in our culture means the institutional church, rather than the flesh-and-blood people of God, has become the vehicle of God's mission in the world. We believe that with the right corporate vision, structures, and policies the institution will be divinely empowered to do Christ's work. The minister's task becomes initiating and managing programs so that spiritual maturity can be cultivated among members. This is salvation via institution, paradise via programs. And preferably *our* programs rather than the church's down the street.

PAVED WITH GOOD INTENTIONS

I thought I was going to vomit. The car was swerving back and forth. "Isn't this amazing?" said Pastor Cliff from the driver's seat as he yanked the steering wheel like a child at an amusement park. "I never could have done this when the parking lot was gravel," he said with a giggle. The car screeched around a curb. Each turn reverberated through the cushy suspension of the Buick. It was like driving a waterbed. As Cliff continued to slalom through the empty parking spaces at high speed, I debated whether he'd be more upset if I puked in his car or on his pristine new asphalt lot.

When the car finally stopped, Cliff's face was beaming with pride. "Have you ever driven on a smoother parking lot in your life?" he asked smugly.

"Nope," I said while removing my fingernails from the dashboard. "That was really great," I lied.

Cliff had been in church ministry for over forty years. The wiry pastor was effortlessly charming and full of energy. It was easy to understand why he'd survived so long in one church. His feisty spirit made me doubt retirement would find him watching sunsets and drinking sweet tea. Cliff was a scrapper, a tough dog to keep on the porch. I immediately liked the old guy, and could embrace him as my pastor if not my driver.

I was visiting Cliff to interview him for an article. Being a young church leader myself, I looked forward to hearing from an elder pastor who had run the race and fought the good fight. Sitting in his office earlier in the day, Cliff reminisced about his career. "Looking back," I asked him, "what are some of your fondest memories of ministry?"

"In thirty-two years I led the church through *five* building campaigns," Cliff said. "Nothing takes it out of you like a building campaign. That's why so many pastors leave after just one. There's money to raise, committees, builders and architects, permits—all kinds of problems. It's not easy. But I made it through *five*. I'm proud of that."

I tried to dig deeper, hoping to find what really motivated Cliff's ministry. "What is it about a building campaign that's so satisfying?" I asked.

"When I came here the church only had 150 people. But we raised the money to buy fifteen acres on the edge of town, and it took us five years to build the new church. It was a real challenge. But I'll never forget that first day in the new building. It was amazing. After that we did it four more times. We added classrooms, a gymnasium, a new roof, and then a larger sanctuary. I'm still amazed at what we've accomplished. And now with the technology," his arms up in the air in disbelief, "we've added monitors in the foyer. Can you imagine! Screens in the foyer!" Cliff was out of his chair with excitement.

At this point I was getting worried. I hadn't flown from Chicago to hear stories about gymnasiums and monitors. I needed *pastor* stories. You know, stories about praying with the town drunk in a jail cell and seeing his life turn around, or unexpectedly weeping at the funeral service for the cranky old lady you secretly wished the Lord had taken years sooner. For the sake of my article as well as my own belief in ministry, I needed to hear *people* stories—some evidence that ministry meant more than managing a facility.

I gave Cliff another chance. "Amid all of that, is there anything that stands out to you? Something you're particularly proud of? Did you see God do something surprising in your people?"

"Oh yeah," he said. "I never thought the elders would come around during this last campaign. I'd been telling them for years that we needed to expand the parking lot, but they didn't believe me. I fought with them for at least two years on that issue. But persistence and prayer paid off; they changed their minds. That new parking lot is beautiful. It's definitely one of my proudest accomplishments." Cliff motioned for me to look out his office window. The gesture was given with the same proud look I've seen from grandparents showing off photos of their grandchildren. I in turn fabricated my same look of genuine interest for Cliff.

"It looks very … smooth," I said.

"Yeah," Cliff replied adoringly. "But to really appreciate it you've got to *feel* it. Come on." The giddy pastor was out the door before I knew what had happened.

Walking toward his car, Cliff launched into a monologue. I could tell it was likely the same presentation he had given to the elders. "Years ago the rule for determining a church's parking lot was simple. You took the average attendance for a Sunday in May or October and divided the number by four. That's how many parking spots you needed. But that doesn't work anymore. More people are driving today. All the consultants now say you should divide the number by two — especially in areas without on-street parking.

"The elders agreed, and three years ago we put in a larger gravel lot, but I knew it wasn't good enough. 'We've got people around here driving BMWs and Cadillacs,' I told them. They don't want to park on gravel. People expect asphalt! A church that can't provide asphalt isn't relevant. It's not credible. Eventually the elders came around. A respectable church simply couldn't ask people to park on gravel.

"We spared no expense. This parking lot is a masterpiece. It's smooth as glass; the best lot of any church in town. Worth every penny. Attendance has gone up 4 percent since it was finished last spring."

The car doors slammed shut, the engine roared, and Cliff was off to the races. He hung over the steering wheel like a pilot searching for a landing strip. I hadn't bothered to fasten my seat belt for what I assumed would be a leisurely cruise around the parking lot. Soon enough my posterior was sliding across the La-Z-Boy size leather seats as Pastor Andretti began warming up the tires.

During my flight home, I wrote in my journal about my experience with Cliff:

Cliff is a delightful man. Warm, caring, talks like a Chatty Cathy doll, loves to tell stories. But after decades of ministry every question came back to the building. It's obvious that Cliff views that building as a tangible symbol of his work as a pastor, a monument to his service to God.

But here is where I find myself—I don't want my legacy to be a building. When I'm sixty-nine years old I don't want my conversations to focus on parking lots and building campaigns. Cliff is a good man. I know there is more to his ministry than I observed today. But he's reminded me that I also want there to be more to my mine.

Your God Is a Gumball Machine

Pharisees such as Nicodemus thrived on theological precision; ambiguity was the enemy and metaphors were unhelpful. This explains, at least in part, why he completely misunderstood when Jesus told him that he must be "born again" to see God's kingdom. "How can a man reenter his mother's womb?" Nicodemus wondered aloud. After telling the literal-minded Pharisee that he was speaking about a spiritual rebirth, not a physical one, Jesus chastised him for being a "teacher of Israel" who failed to understand heavenly things.

Then Jesus tested Nicodemus's understanding with another metaphor for the kingdom, this time wrapped in a pun. Maybe it was windy the night Nicodemus came to Jesus with his questions, I don't know. But Jesus told him, "The wind blows where it wishes, and you hear its sound, but you do not know where it comes from or where it goes. So it is with everyone who is born of the Spirit."[7] (In both Greek and Hebrew the word "wind" also means "breath" and "spirit.")

Jesus was highlighting a central flaw of the Pharisees' worldview: their insistence on religious precision left no room for mystery. The pharisaical view said God worked in a definitive and knowable manner, that his response to every human condition or action was predictable and therefore controllable. For example, according to the Pharisees, wealth was a blessing from God bestowed upon the righteous. Conversely, those in poverty or illness were clearly guilty of sin. Therefore, blessings could be assured through proper self-management and adherence to the laws of God.

This attitude was nothing new. In the ancient world most religion was marked by attempts to control deities and predict their actions. Known as divination, the practice has taken many forms. Markings on the entrails of sacrificed animals were interpreted to determine the gods' actions or predict future events. Astrology was a celestial version of this same practice. Entering alternate states of consciousness to commune with spirits or necromancy, speaking with the dead, are still common among animistic religions today. And it was believed that reciting incantations with a deity's name would allow a person to control the god for his or her own purposes.

While all of these practices were commonplace in the ancient Near East, they were strictly forbidden among the Israelites whose relationship with their God was fundamentally different. Rather than a religion of superstition or divination, attempting to control and manipulate God, the Hebrew Scriptures called them to "love the LORD your God with all your heart and with all your soul and with all your might."[8] Trusting in God's fidelity and goodness, they were to abandon attempts at predicting the future or controlling spiritual powers. After all, if the God of creation has pledged himself to you, why fear the future or the meddling of lesser deities? Besides, any attempt to control the God of Israel, who had already proven his power over the gods and armies of Egypt, was futile to begin with.

For this reason, Israelites who practiced divination were guilty of a terrible sin. They were rejecting the call to love and trust God, and instead attempting to gain power and control over him. They were trying to manipulate God like a puppet on a string to achieve their own purposes. They wanted to make the Infinite into an instrument.

By the time of Jesus, Pharisees were attempting divination by other means. With their mechanical, formulaic view of God, the essence of divination had morphed into a form acceptable to Jewish sensibilities. They sought to contain and control God with their strict adherence to religious laws. Sacrifice A, recite prayer B, abstain from C, and God *will* bless you with D. Outcomes were guaranteed. They made God akin to a divine gumball machine. Insert the correct coin (offer the correct sacrifice), twist the knob (obey the rules), and you will receive your candy (blessing). This is why they put so much energy into determining the precise amount of dill or mint to be tithed, and exactly how long the tassels on their prayer shawls should be. Their intent to precisely follow God's law was not motivated by love, but a desire to manipulate God and control outcomes.

But Jesus says God isn't like a gumball machine; he's more like the wind: unpredictable, uncontrollable, no more containable than wind in a bottle. The wind blows where it wishes, and any attempt to define where it comes from and where it will go is futile. And those who are born of the Spirit will not rigorously focus on defining God's ways to contain and control him, but will humbly submit to the Spirit's unpredictability and happily be carried along on his breath. Nicodemus failed to understand this, Jesus said, because he had never experienced it.

Like the Pharisees and the pagan priests of old, we also want to contain and control God. The 1995 bestseller *Jesus CEO: Using Ancient Wisdom for Visionary Leadership*, by Laurie Beth Jones, is a stark example of modern divination. Jones examines Jesus' management style and deciphers three core principles: self-mastery, action, and relationship skills. She calls these Jesus' "Omega management style," and she believes they apply equally to business, government, or religion. "Anyone who practices these spiritual principles," Jones asserts, "is bound to experience success. In fact, the study and application of spiritual principles comes with success guaranteed."[9]

The exchange of an unpredictable God for controllable principles is also common within the church. Our insistence on an institutional and programmatic faith is a savvy new form of divination. Invariably, churches that experience significant numerical growth will publish books outlining their methodology and create conferences so other leaders can reproduce such success in their own churches. The assumption is that with the right curriculum, the right principles, and the right programs God's Spirit will act to produce the outcomes we desire. This plug-and-play approach to the Christian life makes God a cosmic vending machine, and it assumes his Spirit resides within well-produced organizations and systems rather than people.

This desire to bottle, reproduce, and perpetuate the Spirit's power is often evident after the death or departure of a godly leader. A man or woman powerfully filled with the Spirit's breath accomplishes amazing ministry for Christ. Others are attracted to the leader and over time a community forms. But once the Spirit-filled leader is gone, those remaining assume his or her ministry can and should be perpetuated. The wind may have shifted, but they want it to keep blowing in the same direction. So, an institution is established based on the departed leader's values, methods, and vision. If these are rigorously maintained, it is believed, then the same Spirit-empowered ministry that was evident in the leader's life will continue through the institution that bears his or her name. Many ministries and denominations originated in just this way.

But what we often fail to see is that the Spirit was not unleashed in the leader's life because he or she had the right values or employed the right strategy. This "fire of God," as Dallas Willard calls it, was in their soul because of their intense love of Jesus Christ. Rather than focusing on reproducing a leader's ministry methodology, we ought to focus on reproducing his or her devotion to God, but that is a far more challenging task. We have become experts at replicating systems and programs, but how do you replicate something as mysterious as a soul consumed with the fiery love of Christ? As Willard writes, "One cannot write a recipe for this, for it is a highly personal matter, permitting of much individual variation and freedom. It also is dependent upon grace—that is, upon God acting in our lives to accomplish what we cannot accomplish on our own."[10]

A soul ablaze with divine love cannot be manufactured or mass produced any more than love between a husband and wife or a parent and child. And institutions, despite the personhood ascribed to them in our imaginations, are not capable of love. Real love is something that can only exist between persons. This explains why a relationship between God and his people is at the heart of both the Old and New Testaments, rather than the constructions of religious systems of divination and control. Unlike idols which can be confined and controlled, God describes himself as a consuming fire—unquenchable, uncontrollable, and untamable.

This is what highly institutional Consumer Christianity fails to grasp. It seeks to construct programs to capture God's power and produce predetermined outcomes, rather than surrender to the mysterious movement of God's grace which, like the wind or fire, is beyond our control. And God's Spirit does not empower programs or inhabit institutions. The Spirit fills *people* who were created in God's image to be the vessels of his glory.

THE OTHER SAINT AUGUSTINE

In 1885, Vincent van Gogh enrolled in the Academy of Fine Arts in Antwerp. Despite passing many classes easily, he found the institute stifling. The academy simply could not contain his passion for encountering the raw reality of life. It was too sterile, too programmed. He was given high marks for enthusiasm and vitality, but he missed painting among real people.

It was common for students at the academy to paint skeletons as a way of learning proper form and anatomy. Vincent hated the practice. To him the bones symbolized the lifeless institutional art practiced by the school. As a way to mock the academy and bring a sense of life and spontaneity into his painting, van Gogh inserted a burning cigarette between the skull's teeth. The juvenile prank was not appreciated by his professors, who discredited Vincent's vivid paintings as childish and unprofessional. After a year at the school he could bear no more and left the academy to pursue art among the living.

In 1888, Vincent relocated to the warmth of southern France to paint flowers. He sought to emulate the Japanese style of painting that had captured his imagination at the time. The abundant orchards and blossoming trees around the town of Arles would be the perfect place for Vincent to hone his Asian style. With money from his brother, he rented an old yellow house in town. Flowers had drawn Vincent to Arles but he found himself fascinated by the people he met there, particularly at the café located around the corner from his home. He painted soldiers and shepherds, prostitutes and barmaids, a one-eyed man and a school boy. In Arles he produced a staggering number of portraits. It seemed no matter where Vincent went, or what he intended to paint, his focus invariably returned to the numinous quality of ordinary people. Earlier he had written: "I prefer painting people's eyes to cathedrals, for there is something in the eyes that is not in the cathedral, however solemn and imposing the latter may be—a human soul, be it that of a poor beggar or of a street walker, is more interesting to me."[11]

Van Gogh's closest friend in Arles was Joseph Roulin, the local postman. He painted Roulin many times in his navy blue uniform, hat, and giant beard that parted below his chin. In fact, he painted every member of Roulin's family, but he was particularly captivated by Roulin's wife, Augustine, and their infant son. Vincent always thought highly of family, and the centrality of these relationships was reflected in his art. Whether a husband and wife resting from their labors together on a haystack, a young mother kneeling before a crib, or a couple watching their child take her first step—his paintings celebrated the sacredness of these basic human relationships.

Vincent did a series of five portraits of Augustine Roulin while in Arles. The thirty-seven-year-old mother of three is depicted sitting in a chair, dressed entirely in green. *(See color insert, Image 7.)* Van Gogh's intent for the painting is revealed by a word he painted under her left elbow on the arm of the chair: *La Berceuse* (French for "the cradle-rocker"). In her hand, Augustine holds a rope that leads forward off the edge of the canvas to the unseen cradle she is rocking. Vincent intentionally did not paint the cradle. Instead, the viewer is placed where the cradle should be to look back at Augustine. He hoped the painting would be comforting to all who saw it as they placed themselves in the cradle and experienced again the sacred relationship between a mother and her child.

The soothing moment is made restless, however, by Vincent's characteristically bold use of color. But this also was very intentional on his part. He said, "I want to paint men and women with that something of the eternal which the halo used to symbolize, and which we seek to convey by the actual radiance and vibration of our coloring."[12] Rather than a halo, the background of the painting is dominated by a floral pattern that appears like fireworks behind Augustine's head. The colorful swirling flowers may have been a prototype for the sky Vincent would paint six months later in *Starry Night*. In addition, the jarring use of red and green creates the vibration of color Vincent hoped would convey the presence of holiness. He was elevating this ordinary act of motherhood to a sacred vocation; he was depicting Augustine Roulin as a saint.

Vincent's portraits of Augustine Roulin, along with the many other faces he painted in Arles, stand in bold contrast to his experience at the fine arts academy. He recognized that people were the vessels of God's Spirit, and that love is something transmitted along the medium of relationship. For van Gogh the world of institutional art was a skeleton. It had the form and structure of a human being, but none of the flesh, breath, or feeling that makes someone truly alive. And while locked within the academy, an artist did not experience the full humanity of his calling. He did not relate to his subjects in their world and know them as whole people. They were merely objects of light and color to be replicated on a canvas. But Vincent lived and moved among his subjects. He entered their homes, drank with them at the café, and worked beside them in the fields. This explains why the colors in his paintings evoke such emotion. He wasn't just painting the *person* in front of him; he was painting his *relationship*.

It is no coincidence that van Gogh painted *The Cradle-Rocker* just before Christmas 1888. In letters he acknowledged the symbolism the cradle held for him. "It is a strong and powerful emotion which grips a man when he sits beside the woman he loves with a baby in a cradle near them … it is always the eternal poetry of the Christmas night with the baby in the stable — as the old Dutch painters saw it, and Millet and Breton — a light in the darkness, a star in the dark night."[13] In Jesus' birth he saw God's affirmation of humanity, the sacredness of ordinary people, and the centrality of relationships. After all, the miracle of Christmas was not that God sent a curriculum or birthed an institution, but that he sent his own Son to become flesh and make his dwelling among us. For Vincent the sacred was always incarnate.

SOUL FRIENDS

"Earth shaking." "Ground breaking." "Mind blowing."[14] That is how Bill Hybels, senior pastor of Willow Creek Community Church, described the data that had been laid in front of him. In 2004, the flagship of American megachurches undertook a study of their ministry to determine its effectiveness. Quantitatively, everyone considered Willow Creek a success. One of the largest churches in the country, it had effectively drawn thousands of "unchurched" suburbanites back to the institutional church. But was it really helping people grow spiritually? Was it accomplishing its stated mission of transforming people into fully devoted followers of Christ?

Willow's executive pastor, Greg Hawkins, summarizes the church's program-driven approach this way: "We create a variety of programs and services for people to participate in.... This is our strategy. We try to get folks who are far from God involved in these activities. We believe the more people are participating in these sets of activities with high levels of frequency it will produce disciples of Christ — people characterized by increasing love for God and other people. I know that might sound crazy, but that's how we do it in churches. We measure levels of participation."[15]

Willow Creek's qualitative study was launched to determine whether this assumption is accurate. Do people love God and love others more after regularly participating in the programs of the church? Do institutions produce disciples? Can programs ignite love? The conclusion reached after surveying 15,000 people at Willow Creek and twenty-five other churches was no. Hawkins says: "Increasing levels of participation in these sets of activities does NOT predict whether someone's becoming more of a disciple of Christ. It does NOT predict whether they love God more or they love people more."[16]

When the results were presented to Bill Hybels, he described it as "the wake up call" of his adult life. Presenting the findings to other church leaders, Hybels said: "Some of the stuff that we have put millions of dollars into thinking it would really help our people grow and develop spiritually, when the data actually came back it wasn't helping people that much. Other things that we didn't put that much money into and didn't put much staff against is stuff our people are crying out for."[17]

This may have been the most illuminating conclusion of the study. It showed that most people didn't need elaborate programs or pre-engineered activities to grow in their love of God and others. Following Christ did not require the institutions. "This was difficult to learn," Hawkins says, "because we had viewed ourselves as helping people all along their spiritual journey."[18] But the data showed that the more spiritually mature people became, the more dissatisfied they were with the church. In fact, those recognized to be the most Christ-centered were the least enthusiastic about engaging church programs. Rather than a utilitarian ocean liner transporting them closer to God, the church was seen as a lumbering cruise ship full of entertaining distractions, and the more mature Christians were eager to get off.

The research found that what impacted a person's spiritual growth most were personal Bible reading, prayer and meditation, a meaningful relationship with a friend or mentor, and serving others. None of these practices required a mega institution. In fact, these disciplines have been practiced by Christians throughout the centuries even in places where no organized Christian institution existed at all. And all of these practices are relationship-focused. Meditating upon Scripture and prayer are means of communing with God. And fostering spiritual friendships with other Christian brothers and sisters nourishes the soul in a way that an artificial relationship with a personified institution cannot.

These findings do not indict the church, they do not make the church irrelevant to God's mission, and they do not justify Christians abandoning the church in favor of an individualistic faith. Instead, these findings should make us pause and question the missional validity of turnkey programs organized into an institution we commonly call "the church." As Chris Armstrong says, we must see the church "not as a pragmatic set of programs and organizations to be manipulated by managers into a cash machine for the needs of modern Westerners, but as the powerful, untamable, Spirit-driven, Mysterious Body of which Paul spoke."[19] Properly understood, the church is not an institution. It is the community of Jesus' followers on earth — men, women, and children filled with God's Spirit, living in communion with him, one another, and the world. It is a spiritual and relational entity. And *this* church is critical to the advancement of God's mission in the world and an essential component of our spiritual formation.

This does not mean the church should be unorganized, a fluid and completely unstructured community. Just as our goal should not be to escape consumerism, neither should we abandon institutional churches. This is not a call to ecclesiastical anarchy. In the New Testament we see the earliest Christians organizing their communities to provide for the poor, ensure proper instruction, and extend formative and corrective discipline. Every relational community, like a family, needs structure. But the goal of any structure should be strengthening, not replacing, human relationships which are the medium God uses to carry out his transforming work. The Holy Spirit inhabits human beings, not institutions. Similarly, this is not an indictment of megachurches. Every organizational model has its strengths and weaknesses—from the megachurch to the house church. None are immune from the dehumanizing effects of institutionalization. And none are a structural silver bullet that guarantees healthy relationships with God and neighbor. The goal should not be abandoning one structure in favor of another, but rather fostering the meaningful human relationships through which real ministry happens no matter what church structure we find ourselves within.

This begins by recognizing how our consumer culture has exalted institutions by personifying them in our imaginations, giving them the characteristics of real people. As a result, we don't merely organize institutions to facilitate relationships between people, we organize institutions hoping people will develop relationships with the institution. And the church's mission, to connect people in relationship to Christ, subtly shifts to connecting people in relationship to the institutional church. The influence of consumerism has led us to confuse institutions for people, means for the mission, and programs for the Spirit's power. As Albert Einstein keenly observed, "Perfection of means, and confusion of goals seems, in my opinion, to characterize our age."

One solution being attempted to correct this problem has been a new emphasis upon relational ministry. Institutions and churches are trying to position themselves as the providers of relationships like a match-making service. Mentoring, coaching, accountability and small groups—these programs may result in genuine relationships being formed, but sometimes they are symbolic attempts to enliven the skeleton of Consumer Christianity by putting a cigarette in its mouth. What may be needed is a fundamental rethinking of the church within the minds of the members, cultivating the imagination to conceive of the church as a relational community rather than an institutional organization. Beginning on the smallest end of the scale, this means relearning the lost art of friendship.

Van Gogh's art was transformed when it was set free from the academy and integrated with his life and relationships. I believe this is what we need to counter the disfiguring influence of Consumer Christianity and keep our expectations of institutions in check—Christ-centered relationships with real people. The ancient Celtic Christians believed cultivating these relationships was the core ingredient of the Christian life. They called everyone to have an *anam cara,* a soul friend. This was a spiritual mother or father to guide you in the faith, or a peer to walk beside you on the path of sanctification. This person was a vessel of God's Spirit, welcomed into the closets of your soul to bring light and cleansing. An old Puritan prayer describes these friends as God's "hands and fingers taking hold of me." The Celts believed a Christian without a soul friend was like a body without a head. Let's break free from artificial relationships with unfeeling, uncaring, unloving institutions that cannot contain the unpredictable wind of God's Spirit, and focus instead on building soulish connections with real people filled with the breath of God.

CHAPTER 6

THE LAND OF DESIRE

Through faith we may become "sorrowful yet always
rejoicing" and ever green, and we need not complain
when our youth flies with the maturing of our strength.

Vincent van Gogh

SELLING SANTA

Shortly before Christmas I was walking through Woodfield Mall, the largest in Illinois. I was disappointed to see that Santa's Grotto, where children waited in line for a brief one-on-one consultation with Mr. Claus, had been transformed into an enormous promotional display for the upcoming penguin movie, *Happy Feet*. Apparently the mall's managers were not bothered that Santa was difficult to see among the huge images of computer-generated penguins, and clearly nobody was disturbed by the geographic discrepancy—penguins only live at the South Pole and Santa resides at the North Pole. Sadder to me was the absence of the grand Christmas tree that had stood at the center of the mall since my childhood. It appeared that Santa had sold his season, and his soul, to Warner Brothers Studios. I was comforted by the irony of the scene—the character that had commercialized Christmas a century ago had fallen victim to his own devices.

Christians have always had a strained relationship with Saint Nick. Although his origins are rooted deeply in church lore, his association with the secularization of Christmas has made him persona non grata in many churches. But many of us forget that Christmas itself is a holiday of dubious origin. For example, the Puritans were stridently opposed to the celebration of Christmas. They could find no biblical support for the holiday, and they believed (correctly) that it was originally a pagan festival now masquerading as a Christian one. This view was widely held in America throughout the nineteenth century. In 1855, newspapers in New York reported that Methodist, Baptist, and Presbyterian churches would be closed on Christmas Day because "they do not accept the day as a Holy One." And by the 1860s only eighteen states officially recognized the holiday.

Christmas only gained acceptance among a majority of Protestant Christians when it gained wide acceptance by the American public in general. And that can be attributed to the rise of Santa Claus in the secular pantheon. By the 1920s, Old Saint Nick became a marketing juggernaut for retailers who had embraced Christmas as the premier season for shopping. Church leaders no longer objected to Christmas on the grounds that it was a pagan holiday. Instead their concerns shifted to the ungodly materialism and indulgence of desire they saw being promoted in the name of Christ.

The *New York Times* conducted a survey of Christmas sermons in 1931 and reported a common theme: "the suggestion that Christmas could not survive if Christ were thrust into the background by materialism." Another popular sermon of the period railed that Advent had become little more than a "profit-seeking period."

Sermons about the pagan origins of Christmas or the danger of rampant materialism in Christ's name are unlikely to be heard today. In recent years the dominant message heard from the Christian community during the holiday season has been precisely the opposite. Now it seems many Christians are offended when unchecked materialism in December is *not* explicitly associated with Christ. In 2005, for example, the American Family Association pushed for a boycott of Target stores for not using the words "Merry Christmas" in their seasonal marketing. Like many public institutions, Target opted to use the culturally inclusive phrase "Happy Holidays." That same year, a church in Florida erected a billboard declaring "To HELL with Happy Holidays," hoping to remind motorists that "Jesus is the reason for the season." And anchors on a conservative cable news network launched a "Christmas Under Siege" campaign, exposing businesses and retailers that did not include "Merry Christmas" in their advertising. (The network was selling its own "Holiday Ornaments" on its "Holiday Collection" shopping webpage until bloggers pointed out the hypocrisy.)

In less than a century, Christians have gone from opposing over-consumption at Christmas to demanding it be done in Christ's name alone. The explanation may be in the numbers. Two thirds of the U.S. economy is based on consumer spending, and 50–75 percent of most retailers annual profits are generated during December. This makes the weeks before Christmas the high holy days of consumerism. If Christians engaged the Advent season as they did in generations past, by modeling moderation and self-denial or by ignoring the holiday altogether, it would likely destroy the economy. To ensure economic survival, consumers are stirred into a buying frenzy every winter with the goal of making this year's shopping season more prosperous than the last. Santa Claus has been the mascot of this manipulation since the early twentieth century, but if more Christians have their way the season of shopping will someday be inaugurated by the appearance of Jesus Christ at the end of the Macy's Thanksgiving Day Parade.

DIFFUSION OF DESIRE

Thirty miles from Woodfield Mall, along the river in downtown Chicago are eight huge bronze busts depicting the men responsible for deifying Santa Claus in the consumer pantheon. Most of their last names are familiar to shoppers: Frank Winfield Woolworth, Marshall Field, Aaron Montgomery Ward, John Wanamaker, and Edward Albert Filene are a few. The statues were commissioned to "immortalize outstanding American merchants," and they stand like sentinels outside the Merchandise Mart — at one time the world's largest building and still one of the planet's largest wholesale shopping centers.

These titans of retail are credited with solving one of consumerism's greatest dilemmas: how to convince people to buy products they did not need. With the advent of mass production during the Industrial Revolution, previously unimaginable quantities of goods were being manufactured — far more than the market needed. In order to keep the economic engines running, manufacturers needed a way to artificially increase demand for their products. Advertising was born.

John Wanamaker, who opened Philadelphia's first department store in an abandoned railway depot in 1875, recognized that a thriving industrial economy required consuming products at a pace equal to the rate of manufacturing. People had to purchase more items than they needed more often than they wanted. As a result, Wanamaker believed the goal of business was no longer to manufacture products but to manufacture desire for the products. A pioneer in advertising, you can thank John Wanamaker for those intrusive full-page newspaper ads and the creation of pseudo holidays like Mother's Day. He described the ideal consumer economy as a "land of desire," and his department store as a "garden of merchandise" where those desires could be fulfilled.

A contemporary of Wanamaker, marketing expert Emily Fogg Mead said in 1901 that a successful business needed advertising to ensure the "diffusion of 'desire' throughout the entire population," and "We are not concerned with the ability to pay, but with the ability to want." Mead believed ads convinced the "imagination and emotion to desire."[1] Another advocate of advertising at the time said, "Without imagination, no wants, without wants, no demand to have them supplied."[2]

Ads became the prophets of consumerism—turning the imaginations of the people toward the goods they didn't know they wanted. They subtly or overtly promised more comfort, status, success, happiness, and even sex to people who purchased their wares. In 1897, one newspaper reader said that in the past we "skipped ads unless some want compelled us to read, while now we read to find out what we really want."[3] The ability of advertising to manufacture desire is succinctly illustrated by James Twitchell. "Ponder this: before Listerine there is no mention in popular culture of bad breath."[4]

According to the *New York Times*, every day each American is exposed to 3,500 desire-inducing advertisements, all promising that satisfaction is just one more purchase away. Rodney Clapp says, "The consumer is schooled in insatiability. He or she is never to be satisfied—at least not for long. The consumer is tutored that people basically consist of unmet needs that can be appeased by commodified goods and experiences."[5]

A century of manufacturing insatiable desires has created a culture of overindulgence; obesity, sexual promiscuity, and skyrocketing consumer debt are just a few signs. Although lack of self-control has always plagued humanity, for the first time in history an economic system has been created that relies on it. An economist in 1955 said, "Our enormously productive economy demands that we make consumption our way of life, that we convert the buying and use of goods into rituals, that we seek our spiritual satisfaction, and our ego satisfaction, in consumption."[6]

Fifty years later, if people began suppressing their desires and consuming only what they needed, our economy and society would collapse. To prevent this, the satisfaction of personal desires has become sacrosanct. For example, during World War II the government severely restricted public consumption of certain goods needed for the war effort. Following 9/11 however, Americans were repeatedly told that making any sacrifices to their indulgent lifestyles was tantamount to "letting the terrorists win." Under consumerism, the fulfillment of desire has become the highest good and final arbiter when making decisions—even when deciding where to worship.

It isn't difficult to see the incompatibility of this basic virtue of consumerism with traditional Christianity. Scripture champions contentment and self-control, not the endless pursuit of personal desires. Unfortunately, teaching and modeling these increasingly un-American values is not a high priority in most churches. In fact, many churches are using the same desire-inducing marketing techniques pioneered by merchandisers to draw people through their doors. In his 1988 book, *Marketing the Church*, George Barna chided church leaders who failed to embrace the desire-producing power of advertising: "My contention, based on careful study of data and the activities of American churches, is that the major problem plaguing the church is its failure to embrace a marketing orientation in what has become a market-driven environment."[7]

Over the past twenty years it appears many Christian leaders have heeded Barna's rebuke. Today, marketing strategies and advertising methodology are pervasive in American ministry. As discussed in the previous chapter, churches are in competition with one another for survival. They must convince a sustainable segment of the religious marketplace that their church is "relevant," "comfortable," or "exciting," while at the same time creating a desire for church among a population that does not feel the need. Sometimes this requires appealing to the most basic of human compulsions. A church in Indiana promoted a sermon series about sex with billboards showing two pairs of intertwined feet protruding from a bed sheet. A more juvenile, but equally disturbing, billboard in my area simply proclaims, "Kids love our church. It's FUN!" John Wanamaker would be impressed.

STRANDED IN NEVERLAND

Princesses scare me. It isn't their volatile behavior, creepy stepmothers, or the ferocious fire-breathing beasts that often accompany them that are worrisome. Rather, it's the mind control they have over my daughter.

When Zoe sees a princess her pupils dilate and her head cocks. It's like invisible fairies are whispering spells in her ear. Then she turns to me and says, "Daddy, can we buy that?" I know it isn't really Zoe speaking, but the Disney demon that has temporarily possessed her.

Disney's "Princess" brand campaign was launched in 2000 when the company's new chairman of consumer goods—a former Nike executive—brought together Disney's favorite heroines under one banner. Snow White, Cinderella, Sleeping Beauty, Belle, Jasmine, and Ariel became a marketing dream team generating billions of dollars. They appeared on everything from DVDs to Band-Aids. The Disney spell was cast upon my daughter minutes after she entered the world. The hospital diapers were imprinted with Disney's princesses, and they have been a part of her life happily ever after.

But the company is no longer content having only girls fawning over their animated royals. A *Newsweek* article reports, "If Disney has its way, women will become the next subjects kneeling before its $4 billion throne."[8] They are unrolling a new lineup of products aimed at grownups, including a princess Visa card, princess sheets and towels, princess pajamas, and even princess wedding gowns costing thousands of dollars. The head of Disney's apparel line says, "We want women to have a little bit of princess every day."[9]

You may be asking why any adult would want to get married in a yellow wedding dress resembling Belle's from *Beauty and the Beast*? The answer is found in a consumer culture designed to keep adults thinking, and buying, like children. Maturity and rationality are the enemies of our desire-based economy. As Benjamin Barber says, "For consumer capitalism to prevail you must make kids consumers and make consumers kids."[10]

Disney is working both ends of this equation—first, by marketing its princess products to children so they will nag their parents to buy them, and then by seeking to keep a generation of girls in a state of perpetual immaturity so they won't stop buying their princess-branded goods as adults. Disney wants children, the people most susceptible to desire-inducing ads, to make the spending decisions for the family, and they want adults to continue behaving like children. The ideal consumer remains a child from the womb to the tomb.

Of course Disney is not the only company seeking to delay or even destroy adulthood. The marketing efforts of most corporations do not appeal to rationality but instant gratification. They don't want adults thinking about their purchases, but emotionally spending their income to satisfy immediate desires. We are a culture of binge buying that applauds juvenile behavior. Author J. M. Barrie began his classic book, *Peter Pan*, with the line: "All children, except one, grow up." The powers fueling our consumer culture are trying hard to prove him wrong. Joseph Epstein acknowledges that today more adults are "locked in a high school of the mind, eating dry cereal, watching a vast quantity of television, hoping to make sexual scores" and generally enjoying "perpetual adolescence, cut loose, free of responsibility, without the real pressures that life, that messy business, always exerts."[11]

Formed to avoid responsibility and satisfy desire, statistics reveal more adult children are living with their parents well into their thirties, the average age for marriage has risen steadily among both men and women since 1980, and the age of cosmetic surgery patients is rapidly declining. We have also seen the emergence of a new medical field to give scientific justification to perpetual youth. The American Academy of Anti-Aging Medicine, comprising nearly 12,000 physicians and scientists, denies that "aging is natural and inevitable."[12] Fittingly, the group held their 2008 conference at Walt Disney World.

Psychiatrists, such as M. Scott Peck, author of *The Road Less Traveled*, define maturity as the ability to delay gratification. He writes, "Delaying gratification is a process of scheduling the pain and pleasure of life in such a way as to enhance the pleasure by meeting and experiencing the pain first and getting it over with. It is the only decent way to live."[13] The ability to make rational decisions and delay gratification to maximize future benefits, the very ability discouraged by our consumer culture, is the prescribed road from adolescence to adulthood. But more people are failing to take this journey, opting instead to remain in Neverland indefinitely. The health of our families and society may be suffering as a result, but the corporations are cashing in.

Given the extent to which American Christianity has adopted the methodology of consumerism by appealing to and rewarding desires, we shouldn't be surprised at the spiritual immaturity evident in the American church. To believe that employing consumer methods in the church will produce spiritually mature Christians is delusional thinking akin to expecting a dog to hatch from a chicken's egg.

In his online column, Gordon MacDonald, a pastor for over forty years and author of dozens of books, pondered why our churches are filled with so many infant (immature) Christians. Given the abundance of resources available, why aren't there more mature men and women of God to emulate and celebrate? "What our [evangelical] tradition lacks of late," he writes, "is knowing how to prod and poke people past 'infancy' and into Christian maturity." MacDonald never advances a definite reason, but wonders "what's been going wrong? Bad preaching? Shallow books? Too much emphasis on a problem-solving, self-help kind of faith?"[14] Could it be that the consumer values—both inside and outside the church—which form the uncontested foundation of our preaching, books, and ministries are fundamentally designed to promote puerility and oppose maturity in all of its forms?

Scripture and tradition tell us that formation into the likeness of Christ, also known as spiritual maturity, is not achieved by always getting what we want. It is not a product of seeking immediate gratification. The apostle Paul compares his pursuit of Christ to competing in a race. It's a focused effort of "self-control" and "discipline."[15] And Peter calls us to supplement our faith with "self-control," "steadfastness," and to do this with diligence.[16] Traditionally, the Christian life has been marked by releasing one's desires, submitting to a spiritual mentor or community, and learning to take up the cross and deny oneself. Shepherds guided believers through formative and corrective disciplines—most being activities we would never choose to engage in if left to our desires. These values are not championed in our consumer culture, and they certainly don't prove popular among church shoppers seeking a comfortable religious experience. But surrendering control and embracing self-denial ensured that believers received what they *needed* to mature in Christ, not simply what they *wanted*.

MAKING MUD PIES

While taxiing to the terminal, the cabin of the airplane depressurized. The muggy outside air slapped our faces like dirty wet socks. My wife's face cringed. "What is that smell?" she asked.

"Welcome to India," I replied. I explained to Amanda that she would eventually get used to the smell of one billion people, many impoverished, living in close proximity to each other. What she would never get used to is the sight of it.

She was speechless as we drove through slums of Mumbai that night, astonished by the scenes that passed by her window. Before they had only been images on a television or photos in a magazine. Now they were little children, holding in their hands baseball-sized tumors growing from their abdomens, tapping on her window asking for help. I understood her silence.

On a previous visit I had been walking in New Delhi with my father. We were hoping to catch a break in the traffic when a boy approached us. He was probably six or seven years old, skinny as a rail, and naked but for tattered blue shorts. His legs were stiff and contorted, like a wire hanger twisted upon itself. He waddled on his hands and kneecaps, which were covered with huge calluses from the broken pavement. Like many other times in India, I wanted to close my eyes and pretend people in such misery didn't exist. But this persistent boy wouldn't let me.

We kept walking down the street looking for a gap in the traffic, ignoring the boy and his shouts. "One rupee, please! One rupee!" The little guy was amazingly fast on his kneecaps, managing to stay ahead of us and in our field of vision. Finally, realizing he wasn't going to give up, my father stopped and gave the boy the satisfaction of looking him in the eye.

"What do you want?" he asked.

"One rupee, sir," the boy said while motioning his hand to his mouth and bowing his head in deference. My father laughed.

"How about I give you five rupees?" he said. The boy's submissive countenance suddenly became defiant. He retracted his hand and sneered at us. He thought my father was joking, having a laugh at his expense. After all, no one would willingly give five rupees. The boy started shuffling away, mumbling curses under his breath.

My father reached into his pocket. Hearing the coins jingle, the boy stopped and looked back over his shoulder. My father was holding out a five-rupee coin. He approached the stunned boy and placed the coin into his hand. The boy didn't move or say a word. He just stared at the coin in his hand. We passed him and proceeded to cross the street.

A moment later the shouting resumed, except this time the boy was yelling, "Thank you! Thank you, sir! Bless you!" He raced after us once again—not for more money but to touch my father's feet. He blocked our way and alternated raising his hands with shouts of acclamation and bowing at my father's shoes. He was literally worshiping us and attracting the attention of everyone on the street.

This, I imagine, is how our God sees us—as miserable creatures in desperate need of his help. But rather than asking for what we truly need, rather than desiring what he is able and willing to give, we settle for lesser things. And when God graciously says "no" to our misled desires and instead offers us more, we reject him. We turn away, cursing him under our breath. We simply cannot imagine a God who would give five rupees when all we desire is one. C. S. Lewis says:

> Indeed, if we consider the unblushing promises of reward and the staggering nature of the rewards promised in the Gospels, it would seem that our Lord finds our desires, not too strong, but too weak. We are halfhearted creatures, fooling about with drink and sex and ambition when infinite joy is offered us, like an ignorant child who wants to go on making mud pies in a slum because he cannot imagine what is meant by the offer of a holiday at the sea. We are far too easily pleased.[17]

The dilemma posed by consumerism is not the endless manufacturing of desires, but the temptation to settle for desires far below what we were created for. The forces of marketing have captured our imaginations and convinced us to desire mud pies and sneer at the possibility that greater pleasures even exist. We have been reprogrammed to desire immediate satisfaction rather than infinite satisfaction.

Jesus was once approached on the street by a miserable and crippled beggar. Not a rail-thin boy in tattered shorts, but a rich young man with every earthly comfort. His poverty was spiritual. He asked Jesus, "What must I do to inherit eternal life?" The man was looking for a ritual to perform or a law to fulfill, but Jesus offered him something greater — a relationship.

"Sell all that you have and give to the poor," Jesus said, "and come, follow me."[18] When the young man heard this he became very sad and walked away. He was enormously rich and unwilling to relinquish his desire for wealth to embrace the infinitely more valuable treasure of Christ. We do not desire too much, but too little.

SORROWFUL YET ALWAYS REJOICING

Shortly after van Gogh's father died in March of 1885, Vincent painted a still life featuring his father's open Bible. Behind the massive book stands an extinguished candle, an obvious reference to his father's death. In the foreground is a small French novel with a tattered yellow cover. It seems to cower before the grandeur of the holy book. *(See color insert, Image 8.)*

Many art historians have seen the painting as Vincent's attempt to illustrate the differences between himself and his father, between the old ways of authoritarian religion and the new ways of liberal modernity. Van Gogh's father was a pastor, highly suspicious of new thought, and an outspoken critic of his son's affection for French novels. But this interpretation misses the nuances of the painting, and it forgets the high regard Vincent retained for Scripture despite his growing skepticism of the institutional church. Years later Vincent's friend would testify that "his Dutch brain was afire with the Bible."

A closer look at the painting reveals the Bible is opened to Isaiah chapter 53, the passage describing the mission of the Suffering Servant. The text is a prophecy written seven centuries before Christ, foreshadowing his intense suffering.

> He was despised and rejected by men;
>   a man of sorrows, and acquainted with grief;
> and as one from whom men hide their faces
>   he was despised, and we esteemed him not.
> Surely he has borne our griefs
>   and carried our sorrows;
> yet we esteemed him stricken,
>   smitten by God, and afflicted.
> But he was wounded for our transgressions;
>   he was crushed for our iniquities;
> upon him was the chastisement that brought us peace,
>   and with his stripes we are healed.[19]

Vincent also ensured the title of the paperback novel was clearly visible. *La Joie de Vivre* (*The Joy of Living*) by Émile Zola. On the surface, the suffering of Jesus described in Isaiah 53 and a modern novel called *The Joy of Living* appear to stand in stark contrast. This explains why many have seen the painting as Vincent's rejection of his father's religion in favor of modernity. But the plot of Zola's novel reveals his true intent. The story is about an orphan girl who is abused, betrayed, and rejected by those she serves. Still, the heroine lavishly loves others at great personal sacrifice, and even saves the life of her enemy's child.

Rather than a contrast, Vincent saw Zola's novel as a modern retelling of Isaiah 53 — a contemporary example of a suffering servant who was rejected and despised. But the painting also celebrates a central paradox of Christian faith — that through experiencing loss the servant of God discovers a greater joy. The final line of *The Joy of Living* reads, "She had stripped herself of everything but happiness rang out in her clear laugh." Likewise, Isaiah 53 vividly describes the sorrow and suffering of Jesus, but van Gogh understood that on the other side of his suffering was elation. This, according to the author of Hebrews, is why Jesus accepted his destiny. He endured the cross, despising the shame, "for the joy that was set before him."[20] He persevered through the suffering because he knew a greater delight awaited him. Jesus accepted suffering not because he suppressed his desires but because he sought to maximize them. Sorrow mingled with joy—it was a paradox Vincent learned from studying Scripture, recognized in French literature, and one he would hold to throughout his life.

After being dismissed as a missionary and losing his dream of becoming a pastor, Vincent described the painful season to his brother: "As molting time—when they change their feathers—is for birds, so adversity or misfortune is the difficult time for us human beings. One can stay in it—in that time of molting—one can also emerge renewed."[21] Suffering was not an abnormality to be avoided, but a facet of God's grace to be accepted. It was the way transformation occurred and new life entered. To sacrifice one's immediate desires was how to fulfill one's ultimate desire. It is an irony articulated by the apostle Paul, who wrote, "I count everything as loss because of the surpassing worth of knowing Christ Jesus my Lord. For his sake I have suffered the loss of all things and count them as rubbish, in order that I may gain Christ."[22]

The redemptive affect of sorrow, its power to redirect our desires from the immediate to the infinite, was the subject of an English sermon van Gogh delivered in 1876:

> Sorrow is better than joy ... for by the sadness of the countenance, the heart is made better. Our nature is sorrowful, but for those who have learnt and are learning to look at Jesus Christ, there is always reason to rejoice. It is a good word, that of St. Paul: as being sorrowful yet always rejoicing. For those who believe in Jesus Christ, there is no death or sorrow that is not mixed with hope—no despair—there is only a constant being born again, a constantly going from darkness into light.[23]

Vincent's belief that momentary suffering would lead to perpetual joy was put to the test when he entered the asylum in Saint-Rémy. During this most traumatic period of his life he identified closely with the suffering of Christ. Wandering the countryside near the hospital, he was drawn to the groves of olive trees. Their contorted limbs and gnarled bark reminded him of Jesus' night of agony among the olive trees in the garden of Gethsemane. There, the same night Judas betrayed him, Jesus prayed to his Father concerning the suffering that loomed: "My Father, if it be possible, let this cup pass from me." It was his desire to forego the suffering of the cross. His anguish was so intense that Luke says his sweat was like drops of blood. Jesus' immediate desire was to escape his pain, but it was not his ultimate desire.

After asking his Father to remove the cup Jesus adds, "Nevertheless, not my will, but yours, be done."[24] His truest and deepest desire was to fulfill the will of his Father, and "by becoming obedient to the point of death, even death on a cross," be exalted by God and "given the name that is above every name, so that at the name of Jesus every knee should bow, in heaven and on earth and under the earth."[25] By abandoning his immediate desire, he was indulging his greatest desire — to be glorified above all things. The garden of Gethsemane is where the Suffering Servant reveals the depths of his suffering, but it is paradoxically where he reveals his deepest joy.

Van Gogh painted a number of biblical scenes while being treated in St. Rémy, but he never painted Jesus in Gethsemane. He did attempt to paint the scene once, but then scraped it off and never tried again. Perhaps the complicated interplay of sorrow and joy he recognized in Gethsemane eluded even his artistic brilliance. In 1889, his friends Gauguin and Bernard sent him photographs of their paintings of *Christ in the Garden of Olives*. Vincent said the paintings "got on my nerves" perhaps for the same reason he abandoned his own attempt. They could depict Jesus' suffering, but not the inner joy that led him to accept the Father's will.

Rather than painting Jesus in Gethsemane, Vincent used the olive trees themselves to illustrate the truth of the story. He believed "that one can try to give an impression of anguish without aiming straight at the historic Garden of Gethsemane."[26] Instead, he saw in the contorted trees a representation of Christ's pain. By giving the olive trees a vaguely human form van Gogh hoped to "make people think" more than if he had depicted Jesus explicitly. In this way the trees could be the symbol of Jesus' pain as well as his own. *(See color insert, Image 9.)*

Also a departure from more traditional depictions of Gethsemane is the brightness of Vincent's painting. He does not paint the shadows of a garden at night, but a blazing golden sun. Like so many of his paintings, this one is dominated by yellow, van Gogh's color of divine love. The trees writhing in pain stretch out toward the infinite joy of God. It is a re-rendering of his father's Bible and Zola's novel, and it is an illustration of the contrasting feelings inside the artist's soul. "It is true that I am often in the greatest misery," he wrote, "but still there is a calm pure harmony and music inside me."[27] Van Gogh's *Olive Trees* captures this paradox in paint: we are sorrowful yet always rejoicing.

Know Pain, Know Gain

Self-denial, the surrendering of immediate desires, is a prerequisite of the Christian life. As Dietrich Bonhoeffer so succinctly states, "When Christ calls a man, he bids him come and die."[28] But this invitation is noticeably absent in the gospel of Consumer Christianity. It promises joy and new life, a healthier marriage, more obedient children, a more balanced life, and less anxiety about the future—but nowhere do these promises carry the price of death. Never are we asked to deny ourselves. That is a value utterly at odds with the foundation of consumerism: the sanctity of personal desire.

For people fully formed by consumerism, any God that expects personal sacrifice on the level that Jesus does cannot be seen as benevolent. He would appear more like James Bond's eccentric villain, Goldfinger, who straps us to a table with a laser beam inching toward our midline. "Do you expect me to talk?" 007 nervously asks. "No, Mr. Bond, I expect you to die," replies a self-amused Goldfinger.

Jesus isn't interested in negotiating. He knows that death, the surrendering of our immediate desires, is how we can take hold of an even greater joy. He illustrates this point in a parable (Matthew 13) in which he describes the kingdom of heaven as a treasure hidden in a field. When a man stumbles upon it he covers the treasure, joyfully sells everything he has, and buys the field. Jesus is not calling us to act foolishly, or to abandon our desires. He is calling us to precisely the opposite. Any rational person would release something of little value to gain something of greater value. Jesus is offering us a holiday at the sea, but we must be willing to abandon our mud pies in the slums.

But how are we to do this when the powers, principalities, and authorities of our world are determined to enslave our imaginations and convince us that the treasure in the field doesn't actually exist? How do we learn to elevate our true desires in a society engineered to cultivate false ones and direct our longings toward things that cannot satisfy and pleasures that do not last?

The transformation of our desires happens like all spiritual trans-formation—by following in the steps of Jesus. In a word, I believe the answer is suffering. This kind of pain comes in two varieties—there is suffering we don't choose, which is often referred to in the New Testa-ment as a "trial," and there is suffering we do choose, which we call a "discipline."

The apostle James begins his letter with the same paradox frequently painted by van Gogh: "Count it all joy, my brothers, when you meet trials of various kinds."[29] These trials are painful situations that we do not choose but which come nonetheless. James' call to rejoice is a counterintui-tive response in a culture demanding comfort and immediate satisfaction. But for those with a higher vision, who have seen the hidden treasure, it makes perfect sense. Dallas Willard writes:

> It is absolutely essential to our growth into the "mind" of Jesus that we accept the "trials" of ordinary existence as the place where we are to experience and find the reign of God-with-us as actual reality. We are not to try to get in a position to avoid trials. And we are not to "cata-strophize" and declare the "end of the world" when things happen.[30]

The "trials of ordinary existence" are the divine curricula for spiritual maturity. These are the laser beams God uses to put our old self with its misappropriated desires to death, and then resurrect a new self with new desires focused on a more lasting joy.

Beyond accepting the cups of suffering offered to us, we are also called to ingest smaller doses of suffering in the form of spiritual disciplines. Disciplines are structured activities that conflict with our base desires. By definition they are not things we naturally desire to do, because once a discipline becomes automatic to our nature it ceases to be a discipline. For example, in grade school I had enormous difficulty learning to read. I did not like doing homework. I would have rather watched *Transformers* cartoons every afternoon. For me reading was a discipline. But because I persevered through homework and accepted the suffering of neglecting my immediate animated desires, reading has ceased to be a discipline for me. Now I do it automatically without effort and I even enjoy it. Disciplines teach us to overcome the temptation to gratify our immediate desires so that we may attain a higher one.

While fasting in the wilderness for forty days, Jesus articulated this reality when he was tempted to turn stones into bread. He said, "Man shall not live by bread alone, but by every word that comes from the mouth of God."[31] Disciplines help us see that our immediate "felt needs" are not the most important. We are more than our base desires, and our lives are not sustained by gratifying them. Despite what advertisers tell us, we do not live by satisfying our desires for food, sleep, comfort, sex, power, status, or beauty. We live because it is God's will, and the Christian's greatest desire, like Jesus', ought to be conforming to it. "Not my will, but yours, be done." Fasting is one discipline that trains us to see past our felt needs and acknowledge our real needs. It redirects our attention from our immediate desire which is fleeting, to our inner desire which is unending.

Although fasting may be practiced in many ways—including the customary method of depriving oneself of food—in a digital age in which we are assaulted by 3,500 desire-inducing ads every day, perhaps a new form of the discipline is warranted for Christians: the media fast. The benefits of unplugging from the media for a predetermined amount of time are too numerous to list, but let me briefly mention just two. First, a media fast can function like detox for our souls. Remember, the goal of consumerism for the last century has been the diffusion of desire throughout the population, and this mission has been accomplished through the media. By turning off the television, radio, and computer we stop the influx of poison that keeps us buying and desiring more.

Second, and perhaps more importantly, a media fast creates opportunity in our lives to search again for the hidden treasure we first stumbled upon long ago. Consider how much time and mental space you would have to commune with God by simply turning off the screens you stare at most of the day. Rather than being stoked by marketers to desire things that do not satisfy, you could have your imagination illuminated to seek a higher joy by the one who says:

Come, everyone who thirsts,
    come to the waters;
and he who has no money,
    come, buy and eat!
Come, buy wine and milk
    without money and without price.

Why do you spend your money for that which is not bread,
  and your labor for that which does not satisfy?
Listen diligently to me, and eat what is good,
  and delight yourselves in rich food.
Incline your ear, and come to me;
  hear, that your soul may live.[32]

Whether by trials of circumstance or by disciplines of choice, we cannot escape our calling to suffer with Christ. We are invited to follow in the steps of the Suffering Servant, who indulged his deepest desire and pursued eternal joy by embracing the temporary pain of the cross. Although the forces of consumerism would have us remain forever in Neverland by running after every product promising to satisfy our desire and alleviate our suffering, the invitation of Christ is precisely the opposite. The gospel calls us to embrace the paradox of pain by taking up the cross, and under its heavy beam discover the object of our greatest desire — God himself.

CHAPTER 7

A Refuge for Many

*A sincere and true love is a blessing, I think, though
that doesn't prevent occasional hard times.*

Vincent van Gogh

ABANDON SHIP

My daughter thinks I am Superman, and I don't mean metaphorically. She literally thinks I am the Man of Steel. She's even told her friends at preschool my not-so-secret identity. Never mind that I'm bald with a physique that says "Clark Bar" more than "Clark Kent" — Zoe believes her dad can do anything. She got this idea when I arrived home from church much earlier than she did despite leaving at the same time in separate cars. "How did you get home so fast, Dad?" she asked. I unbuttoned my shirt to reveal a Superman shield underneath. Her eyes became saucers. "Wow," she said. I've never bothered to correct her perception. I figure time will handle that.

I suppose many children have believed their fathers possess near infinite capabilities at some point. If I ever believed such a thing about my dad I don't remember it. That's not to say he didn't posses amazing abilities, only that as a child I recognized his powers were finite in scope. Because he's a doctor I saw him leap to the rescue of a heart attack victim in a restaurant or airplane more than once. But throw a domestic problem at him and he withered like Superman before Kryptonite. To be fair, the man always made a valiant effort with the powers he had. Leaky pipes were set and wrapped with a fiberglass cast. A broken vacuum cleaner handle was mended with a splint. Withering house plants were fed nitrates from an IV.

Given the limited applications for my father's powers, you can understand why at age thirteen I wasn't excited about his plan to take sailing lessons together on Lake Michigan. He had arranged for us, along with my older brother and two cousins, to spend three days sailing with an instructor. When we arrived at Belmont Harbor in Chicago my father's confidence was incongruent with a man whose only previous sailing experience had been the log ride at Six Flags. Still, the first two days of instruction went relatively smoothly after my brother discovered why the horizontal mast is called a "boom."

At the end of our third day, the instructor announced the details of our final exam. We were to successfully navigate the sailboat out of the congested harbor, into the open waters of Lake Michigan and back—alone. The instructor would stay ashore this time and monitor our progress. I knew the moment he said "alone" there was no chance I was getting into the boat with only my dad in control. He might as well have asked us to fly a 747. After a short argument with my dad and some teasing from my brother and cousins for being a chicken, they piled into the boat without hesitation (although I saw my brother check his lifejacket buckle more than once) while I stood with the instructor on the pier as they prepared to shove off.

The decision to abandon my shipmates was soon vindicated. The instructor was horrified as the tiny craft bounced around Belmont Harbor like a buoyant pinball. The sailboat seemed magnetically attracted to every object in the water—piers, buoys, other vessels. All the while my dad stood at the helm maintaining a calm command of his crew as if the chaos he was stirring in the harbor was completely normal. Other boats tried to give him a wide berth, and boats tied to piers began hanging extra bumpers over the side hoping to protect their aquatic investments from my father's wind-powered torpedo.

On shore a small group of spectators assembled. At first they were simply curious about the shouts coming from the harbor. *Was someone injured? Was there an accident?* No. The shouts were from boat owners yelling at my dad to keep away from their floating egos. The crowd began pointing and laughing at the ship of fools. Pretending I had no idea who the idiots in the sailboat were, I joined the crowd by laughing and pointing, all the while immensely thankful I was not in the boat with them. (Thirteen-year-olds can handle only so much embarrassment.) Still, I felt a tinge of shame for abandoning my family. The shore was comfortable and safe, but it was lonely.

My dad, brother, and cousins never did make it out of the harbor. Eventually the instructor decided to intervene and rescue the bunch before any more damage was inflicted. As they disembarked, exhausted from their ill-fated trip, I had the satisfaction of telling my brother and cousins, "I told you so." But they carried a different satisfaction—the kind that comes from sharing a common struggle even amid defeat.

Decisions, Decisions

We are very fickle about community. When things are going well, we're eager to jump into the boat and join the fun. But when community requires sacrifice, perseverance, or hard work, we can find ourselves on the shore acting like we don't know those crazy people in the boat. Through the influence of our consumer culture, with its emphasis on immediate gratification, combined with our innate selfishness, many of us approach church the same way. We make calculated decisions about which community will offer the most comfortable environment, and our commitment to that group lasts only as long as the comfort endures. With these values in hand, we decide whose boat we will get into, and whose we'd rather ridicule from the shore. This is the tension that exists in a consumer society. It's the tension between choice and commitment, between comfort and community.

When I arrived at Starbucks to meet with Greg and Margaret, two members of my church, I first went to the counter to order a drink. The relatively simple menu on the wall is deceptive. There was a time when ordering coffee meant regular or decaf, cream or sugar. Today, Starbucks provides literally 20,000 beverage permutations—although the number is much smaller for those of us who consume only tea. I finally ordered a tall Earl Grey nonfat tea misto.

While enjoying our drinks of choice, Greg and Margaret proceeded to explain why they were leaving our church to attend another congregation in a nearby town. The new church, they said, had multiple services on Saturday and Sunday so they could choose to worship at a time that fit their busy schedules. (Our church had only three services—all on Sunday morning.) The youth group had multiple worship teams for their daughter to serve on. (Our student ministry had only one worship team.) And, because it was "way bigger" than our church, it had more to offer Greg and Margaret too. They could find a class or small group that perfectly fit their needs. Despite making a public commitment as members a few years earlier, Greg and Margaret's commitment to our church had ended. A more comfortable ship had sailed into port—one that offered more choices.

A core characteristic of consumerism is freedom of choice. Customization, creating a product that conforms to my particular desires, has driven businesses to offer an ever-increasing number of choices to consumers. Nothing represents this trend better than the iPod. No longer must a listener commit to buy an entire album to enjoy just one song. She now has instant access to millions of songs, and may choose to download them individually to create a personalized playlist. The consumer chooses precisely what she likes, and dismisses what she doesn't.

But there is more to choice than just convenience. As discussed in chapter three, in a consumer society people construct and express their identity through their purchases. By being offered more choices, consumers are better able to construct their own unique identity. Consider Nike's online shop that allows consumers to customize their shoes, appropriately called Nike iD. The website says, "Nike iD was created to reflect your individuality. Nikeid.com + Your Personality = Customization." Starbucks is also pushing customization as a form of identity construction. A small pamphlet at their stores titled "Make It Your Drink" teaches customers how to order a beverage that fits their tastes, but the pamphlet takes it a step further by inviting consumers to order a custom T-shirt imprinted with their favorite drink recipe/identity.

The value being emphasized by these seemingly innocuous examples is pervasive today: the world will accommodate to your desires. You shouldn't settle for anything less than the fulfillment of your precise expectations. Years ago, Henry Ford declared his Model-T automobile was available in whatever color people liked as long as it was black. Today, the Nike iD site declares, "The days of picking things directly off the shelves, or ordering off the menu as it appears, are over." Individuality is the new conformity.

As we've seen repeatedly, the values of consumerism always leak into the church. The demand for choices is no exception. For example, one large church in California has pioneered "video venues"—a trend rapidly gaining popularity among North American churches. Upon entering on Sunday, each family member can choose the worship setting that fits their personal desire and makes them most comfortable. Simultaneously, Grandma can sing hymns in the traditional service, Mom and Dad can enjoy coffee and bagels in the worship café, and the teenagers can lose their hearing in the rock venue. Worshipers no longer have to tolerate music, prayers, or people they don't like. The value of family and congregational unity is drowned out by consumerism's mantra of individual choice. Customization has replaced community as a core value of worship.

"The inspiration for what this church is doing," reports one journalist, "comes from a place where freedom of choice and variety are celebrated: the American shopping mall."[1] The pastor of the video venue church said, "I am very comfortable with a consumer mindset and use that tool to help reach people."[2] But he also recognizes that elevating the value of personal choice results in homogeneous congregations. "Rather than asking everyone to gather for a blended service, we've emphasized and honored our differences by providing a wide variety of worship venues, each targeted at a specific homogeneous group. At present, our people can choose from eighteen different worship options each weekend based on worship style, time slot, or location."[3]

We should hardly be surprised that where the church adopts the values of consumerism homogeneity is the outcome. When given the choice, most people will pick a community that conforms to their style, perspective, lifestage, and ethnicity. Birds of a feather, as the cliché goes, flock together. Church consultant Win Arn says, "Churches grow, and grow best, in their own homogeneous unit ... [and, in addition] people want their pastor to be 'like' them. Not too far above or below, not too far ahead or behind."[4] Essentially, people will choose a church that is comfortable. And comfort is achieved when the pews and pulpit are occupied by people "just like me." This principle has been codified for two generations of church leaders as the "Homogeneous Church Growth Principle."

Greg and Margaret were relatively comfortable at my church. They connected with the people—mostly. And they like the music—usually. But when a larger church presented more options to satisfy the diverse interests of their family, and the possibility of choosing a community group that would more perfectly fit their individual identities, they jumped ship. Whatever diversity they had experienced in our community was abandoned for the chance to have a more homogenous and customized spiritual experience. Choice trumped commitment. Comfort trumped community.

TABLE MANNERS

Imagine New York, Hollywood, and Las Vegas merged into one mega-city. That's how one historian described the ancient Greek city of Corinth. It was, like New York, a center of commerce, like Hollywood, a center of culture, and like Las Vegas, a center of immorality. Corinth's reputation, and its location along trade routes, made it a metropolis attracting diverse people from all over the Roman world. The upper class enjoyed all the luxuries of commerce, and the lower class suffered the indignity of slavery and poverty. It was in this setting that the apostle Paul planted a church.

The struggling community of Christ-followers in Corinth suffered from one habitual problem—they uncritically allowed the values of their culture into the church. The infamous sexual immorality of Corinth entered the church, as did Greek philosophy, and the racial and economic divisions of the city. Hearing reports of immorality and divisions among the church he had fathered, Paul was enraged and heartbroken. His children in Corinth had forsaken the values of Christ for the values of their culture. Paul's first letter to the Corinthians is full of stinging rebukes and calls for repentance. He reminded them that the world's wisdom is foolishness to God, and he called for the immediate cessation of sexual immorality. But Paul's most powerful and condemning words were not directed at the Corinthians' doctrine or sexual behavior, but their table manners.

The early Christians celebrated the Lord's Supper by gathering for a communal meal in a home. Of course there were no church buildings or cathedrals, but like Christians today they assembled on Sundays. And here is where the problem arose. In the Roman world Sunday was not a day off from work. As a result, the wealthier members of the Corinthian church could gather early in the day because their work obligations were flexible or nonexistent. The poorer members of the church—the laborers, servants, and slaves—arrived much later in the evening, typically to discover that the wealthier Christians had already consumed all the wine and eaten the best food. Only the scraps remained for the poorer Christians to glean.

Upon hearing reports of their inconsiderate behavior, Paul responded with outrage. "When you come together, it is not the Lord's supper that you eat. For in eating, each one goes ahead with his own meal. One goes hungry, another gets drunk. What! Do you not have houses to eat and drink in? Or do you despise the church of God and humiliate those who have nothing?"[5]

It had not occurred to the Corinthians that their behavior was inappropriate. In Corinth the rich and poor did not share meals together. They did not sit as equals around the same table. This mentality was carried into the church to effectively create two churches—one fellowship for the rich and another for the poor. The Lord's Supper, an event intended to display the unity of God's people, was being used to reflect the divisions of the world.

Homogeneity. The rich ate with the rich, and the poor ate with the poor. It was the comfortable, normal, and accepted practice in Corinth, and the Corinthian Christians could not imagine living any differently. But Paul could. His view of community was not shaped by the popular values of the day. Paul advocated a radically countercultural idea—unity that transcended the divisions of society.

Like the Corinthians, our imaginations have been captured by the popular methodology of our culture. Homogeneity, fueled by our consumer demand for choice, has led to divisions in the church. Rather than challenging the social divisions of our culture, the church has capitulated to them. Rather than defending the radical imaginations of Jesus and his apostles, who called for unity that transcended the dividing walls of culture, ethnicity, and economics, the Consumer Church has enthusiastically defended the status quo. In the first century, Paul rebuked the Corinthians for their shameful display of disunity around the table of Christ. Had the Corinthians lived twenty centuries later, they would have been praised for offering flexible gathering times and forming homogeneous affinity groups. Ironically, after most other institutions abandoned it, the church continues to be a strong supporter of the pragmatic but erroneous "separate but equal" doctrine.

There is little doubt why we have adopted this posture. In Consumer Christianity, our concern is not primarily whether people are transformed to reflect the countercultural values of God's kingdom, but whether they are satisfied—often measured by attendance and giving. An unhappy church member, like an unhappy customer, will find satisfaction someplace else. As one pastor enthusiastically said, "The problem with blended services is that half the people are happy half the time. But by offering multiple homogenous options, you can say, 'If you don't like this service style, try another one!'"[6]

THE YELLOW HOUSE

Like many artists, van Gogh felt misunderstood. It seemed that every community he entered eventually found his passion intolerable. This proved to be the case with the art academy, the church, and even his family. Still, Vincent longed for a community where his passions could be expressed and encouraged even if they were not entirely shared.

Van Gogh experienced a foretaste of such a community while living with his brother in Paris from 1886–1888. Theo van Gogh was an art dealer and one of the few members of Vincent's family to encourage his painting. Through Theo's many connections in the Parisian art scene, Vincent became acquainted with other emerging painters like Henri de Toulouse-Lautrec, Emile Bernard, and Paul Gauguin. Many of these young, and still relatively unknown, artists were experimenting with new forms and disrupting the art establishment with their work. Vincent loved it. Learning from them, his style matured and grew beyond the earthy portraits of his Dutch period. It was in Paris that van Gogh first began to formulate the idea of starting a studio, a place where fringe artists might "live and paint together—different in individual style but sharing a common aim, exchanging ideas, commenting on each other's work."[7]

With Theo's financial support, Vincent left Paris for southern France where he rented a vacant house on a square in Arles. The four-room house was vacant for a reason. It had no gas for cooking, the bathroom was next door, and it was in poor condition—but the price was right. Vincent enthusiastically moved his few possessions and paints into the home. Despite the house's state of disrepair, van Gogh immediately saw its potential to become the base for his "Studio of the South." He envisioned the studio in religious terms, calling the artists who might live with him "Apostles of Art." He even bought twelve chairs to furnish the home. Fittingly, Vincent's house was bright yellow, a mark of divinity and love in his paintings. "The Yellow House," as he always called it, became a symbol of unity, community, and mission for Vincent. (See color insert, Image 10.)

Theo paid Gauguin, whose art he brokered, a stipend to relocate to Arles and help Vincent launch the studio. When informed of the possibility that Gauguin would join him, van Gogh became giddy. Suffering from loneliness, he was as excited about having a companion as he was about the opportunity to begin his studio. He wrote to Theo: "Do you realize that if we get Gauguin, we are at the beginning of a very great thing, which will open a new era for us?"[8] The romantic idea of an artist community had overtaken him. He spoke of the studio with missionary zeal. It was to be a monastery with Gauguin as its abbot, a place of inspiration for itinerant painters, and "a living force." Through the Studio of the South, van Gogh believed a new school of art would emerge to enlighten the world.

Beyond this outward mission, Vincent also saw the Yellow House as a place of healing for progressive artists who suffered from alienation and the stigma of being unconventional—something van Gogh knew well. Writing to Gauguin before his arrival, Vincent said, "I must tell you that even while working I think continually about the plan of setting up a studio in which you and I will be permanent residents, but which both of us want to turn into a shelter and refuge for friends, against the times when they find that the struggle is getting too much for them." It seems clear that Vincent was projecting his own need for a healing community upon others. Nonetheless, his great desire was for the Yellow House to "become a refuge for many."[9]

Gauguin arrived in Arles on October 20, 1888. The two men spent the days painting inside the Yellow House, in the cafes and streets of Arles, and in the surrounding countryside. They often bickered about painting styles, and Gauguin's domineering personality and arrogance soon made Vincent feel inferior. He responded with outbursts of his own erratic behavior. Van Gogh's idyllic vision of artists living in communal harmony looked more like a contentious episode of a reality television show.

Within weeks it became obvious to Gauguin that the arrangement could not endure. He wrote to Theo, "Vincent and I are absolutely unable to live side by side without trouble caused by incompatibility of temperament and he like I needs tranquility for his work. He is a man of remarkable intelligence whom I esteem greatly, and I leave with regret, but it is necessary."[10] Vincent suspected that Gauguin was planning to leave. The thought of abandonment and returning to isolation was too much for his fragile mind. On the night of December 23, the friends argued at a café. Gauguin refused to return to the Yellow House with Vincent and instead went to a hotel. Devastated, Vincent returned to the Yellow House and severed part of his ear with a razor.

The police found him the next morning in a pool of blood. Vincent awoke at the hospital in Arles shocked at what had happened and with no memory of the event. The emotional stress of losing Gauguin, the gap between his dream of community and its dismal reality, had triggered his first psychotic episode. (Later biographers would argue that van Gogh was schizophrenic or manic-depressive, and unfortunately these ideas have shaped popular opinion about the artist. But Vincent's own physicians, as well as later medical experts, diagnosed him with a form of psychomotor epilepsy. Van Gogh was not insane. The evidence suggests he suffered from seizures in the temporal-lobe of his brain that caused self-mutilation and loss of consciousness.)

Van Gogh's dream of living in a community of artists was over. His newly diagnosed mental illness meant he would be joining a different sort of community—a mental hospital in Saint-Rémy. Still, despite the extreme example, many of us can relate to Vincent's dilemma. He sensed that in community more could be achieved, more could be learned. And in community those who feel isolated and marginalized could find a refuge of healing through acceptance and mutual encouragement. But the idea of community always appears more beautiful than the reality. Real people are difficult, and real arguments erupt. This is the dilemma of community—we desire it, we need it, but we seem ill equipped to create it.

The gap that always exists between the ideal and the reality may be why so many are now abandoning community altogether. They are dismissing the imagination of Jesus Christ who prayed that his followers "may all be one, just as you, Father, are in me, and I in you, that they also may be in us, so that the world may believe."[11] They are dismissing the words written by Paul as sentimental and impractical: "There is neither Jew nor Greek, there is neither slave nor free, there is no male and female, for you are all one in Christ Jesus."[12] And in the vacuum left in our imaginations the conventional ideas of our consumer culture come rushing in. We opt for homogenous gatherings based on individual comfort, rather than the more challenging task of forming real, if flawed, communities in Christ, a healing refuge in a world of division. And so, like Vincent's vacant Yellow House, the church stands as a constant reminder to us of the community that could have been—a worthy dream barely attempted before being abandoned for easier endeavors.

Island of Misfits

"Eleven o'clock Sunday morning is the most segregated hour in America." I used that provocative quote from Martin Luther King Jr. as I began the Sunday school class. I asked the group of white suburbanites what they thought about the statement and then waited for a response.

I was nervous. It was my first day teaching at the church as a seminary intern. I was unknown to the congregation and an untested teacher. To make matters worse, everyone in the classroom was easily twice my age. The pastor had assigned me to teach the book of 1 Corinthians for six weeks in the "Primetimers" class — a name that probably described the group twenty years before I taught the class.

Before diving into the first chapter of the epistle, I wrote my name on the whiteboard and briefly introduced myself to the empty-nesters. "How old are you?" asked a woman in the front row.

"Twenty-five," I replied.

"I've got a daughter about your age. Are you married?"

"Yes, I am." She seemed disappointed.

"What kind of name is Skye?" asked another woman in a polite and inquisitive tone. That was a question I received a lot. I issued my standard explanation.

"Skye is a nickname. My given name is Akash. It's a Hindi name that means 'sky' in English."

"Oh, you're Indian," someone concluded.

"Well, my father is from India," I clarified, "but my mother is Anglo-American. My middle name is Charles, my maternal grandfather's name." A number in the class gave a polite nod. It was the same look a server receives as he explains the special of the day even though the customers have no intention of ordering it.

With my genealogy unpacked, I began the day's lesson. The letter of 1 Corinthians begins with Paul addressing the presence of divisions within the church. Looking for a contemporary connection, I put Martin Luther King's quote before the group. (A quote, by the way, more accurately attributed to Billy Graham who wrote the statement in a *Reader's Digest* article years before it was borrowed by his friend, Reverend King.) " 'Eleven o'clock Sunday morning is the most segregated hour in America.' What do you think about that statement?" I asked.

The long, awkward silence was finally broken by a man in the back row. "I think that statement is absolutely true," he said. "I think it's true, and I think it's good."

I wasn't sure what I had just heard. *Did this guy just say racial segregation in the church is good?* I froze. Every set of bifocaled eyes was staring at me. I didn't know what to do. I scanned the room hoping another student would speak and rescue me from the spotlight. No one did. Then I remembered my training: when you don't know what to say, delay by asking a clarifying question.

"Okay," I said, "can you explain what you mean?"

"Well, the way I read Scripture," he began, "we are all going to be separate around the throne of God in heaven—every nation, tribe, and race, right? So, why shouldn't we all be separate down here?"

My plan had backfired. I was still speechless, and even more shocked than before. I wasn't struck by the man's complete misinterpretation of Revelation, or that a racist still lived forty years after desegregation and 400 miles north of the Mason-Dixon Line. I was speechless because just two minutes earlier I had explained my own biracial heritage to the class. I felt a conflicting surge of fear and anger pass over me. Had the anger won, I would have shot back at the man with pointed questions. *Where around God's throne will I be? What race do I belong to? Or is there a special place for people like me, an island of misfits somewhere outside the pearly gates—a purgatory for half-bloods?*

But my fear was stronger than my anger that day. I remained silent, flipped through my notes, and eventually preceded with the lesson. Later in the hour, as the class talked in small groups, I contemplated how I might get out of teaching the Primetimers for another five weeks. If I explained the situation to the pastor, surely he would understand. He couldn't expect me to keep teaching in such an environment. I needed to be with people who shared more of my values, or people who were at least open to them. And what was I going to do with Bull Conner in the back row? I couldn't avoid calling on him for five weeks. I needed an escape plan. This community had quickly become uncomfortable.

On Monday I met with the pastor. I explained my concerns and he empathically listened. I did not explicitly ask to be transferred to another class. I assumed after hearing my story the pastor would come to that recommendation on his own.

"You're teaching 1 Corinthians, right?" he asked.

"Yeah," I said.

"Unity in the church?" he asked.

"Right," I replied.

"Well, this sounds like a wonderful opportunity for you to practice what you teach." The pastor went on to explain Bull's background. (Bull was what I called the racist; it's not his actual name.) "He grew up in a very different time than you, and in a place that doesn't share your values. You are going to have to find a way to teach that class, challenge his ideas, and stay in community with him."

Of course he was right. I had been so focused on retreating to a more comfortable setting that I couldn't see the hypocrisy of my own desires. Henri Nouwen once observed, "Community is the place where the person you least want to live with always lives." When we abandon ship because it holds people we don't like, we also abandon community. It occurred to me that if I left the Primetimers class to preserve my comfort, I would have no right teaching 1 Corinthians to anyone else. I was going to have to face Bull Conner in the ring of community.

During the weeks I taught the Primetimers class, I challenged Bull in his thinking, and I did my best to hear his perspective. But I came to recognize that his ungodly values were matched by my own. Without knowing it, he helped me understand how my views about community had been shaped by my consumer expectation for comfort, just like Bull's views about community had been shaped by his culture's belief in segregation. We were contaminated by the same disease; we just presented different symptoms. Persevering through that class illuminated the truth about me, and I hope my teaching from 1 Corinthians helped Bull see the truth about him. Writing about the nature of Christian community Nouwen says:

> Community has little to do with mutual compatibility. Similarities in educational background, psychological make-up, or social status can bring us together, but they can never be the basis for community. Community is grounded in God, who calls us together, and not in the attractiveness of people to each other. There are many groups that have been formed to protect their own interests, to defend their own status, or to promote their own causes, but none of these is a Christian community. Instead of breaking through the walls of fear and creating new space for God, they close themselves to real or imaginary intruders. The mystery of community is precisely that it embraces all people, whatever their individual differences may be, and allows them to live together as brothers and sisters of Christ and sons and daughters of his heavenly Father.[13]

A HEAVENLY APPETIZER

Bull's biblical rationale for segregation was completely bogus. He incorrectly read Revelation 7:9 to mean that God's coming kingdom would be segregated, but he did have one part correct. Bull rightly sensed that the future should be reflected in the church today. But the vision recorded by the apostle John was not one of multiple homogeneous communities around the throne of God. It was a vision of unity and integration—a single community that transcended the divisions of the world.

> After this I looked, and behold, a great multitude that no one could number, from every nation, from all tribes and peoples and languages, standing before the throne and before the Lamb.[14]

This vision of unity that transcends worldly divisions has been lost in Consumer Christianity. Instead, it has adopted the pragmatic vision of homogeneity. Working to establish a community that crosses cultural barriers is too difficult, and it is largely unappealing to comfort-driven church shoppers. It is far easier to attract finicky consumers to a church that won't challenge their value of comfort or, better yet, one that will allow them to customize their church experience to fit their unique desires. And while few Christians will deny the value of diversity and community outright, for most it simply doesn't rise high enough in their hierarchy of values to be a factor.

Consumerism has focused us so fully on the individual, that we've lost the corporate and social dimension of the gospel. We have forgotten that part of what Christ accomplished through the cross was not only the reconciliation of individuals to God, but also the reconciliation of estranged people groups to one another. In Ephesians 2, Paul even speaks of human reconciliation as occurring concurrently with divine reconciliation. Christ's purpose "was to create in himself one new man in place of the two, so making peace, and might reconcile us both to God in one body through the cross."[15] And elsewhere Paul obliterates the popular social categories of his day. "Here there is not Greek and Jew, circumcised and uncircumcised, barbarian, Scythian, slave, free; but Christ is all, and in all."[16]

Paul's disregard for social categories, and his unwavering belief in unity through the cross, explains why he was so irate with the Corinthians. By valuing homogeneity more than unity they were contradicting the meaning of the meal. They were contradicting the cross of Christ. Rather than gathering to reflect the heavenly unity of God's kingdom, they gathered to reflect the fallen segregation of Corinth.

If we are to awaken the Christian imagination to the corporate dimension of Jesus' reconciling work, then we must recapture the symbolic power of the table. The table of Christ confronts and abolishes our consumer tendencies. It mocks our desire for comfortable community, and it abolishes the principle of homogeneity because we come to the table of Christ as guests and not the host. We have no control or authority over who is invited. Instead we are asked to surrender control and simply take our seat with the other wounded souls redeemed by the broken body and shed blood of Jesus. His table is a refuge for many, a place to encounter grace at the times when the struggle is getting too hard. But at his table we will probably find the person we like least, and this is the person we are called to love. At the table we not only encounter the living Christ through the bread and wine, but also through the brothers and sisters seated around us. As C. S. Lewis observed:

> Next to the blessed sacrament itself, your neighbor is the holiest object presented to your senses. If they are your Christian neighbor, they are holy in almost the same way, for in them Christ, glorified Himself, is truly hidden.[17]

After chiding the Corinthians for the comfortable manner in which they took the Lord's Supper, Paul challenged them to carefully examine themselves before coming to the table and to wait for one another before eating. Paul desired for all to be present, both rich and poor, so that the table could be a prophetic symbol of Christ's body. He wanted the gathering of believers to be a reflection of God's kingdom, not a reflection of Corinthian culture. It is this prophetic power of the table that can stir our imaginations to not only envision the future reality of the kingdom, but also inspire us to live counterculturally today. Paul Bradshaw has written about the prophetic purpose of the table among the early Christians:

> This meal was a sign of their reconciliation to God and their membership among the elect who would one day feast together in God's kingdom, and the intimate fellowship with one another that they experienced around the table was a foretaste, an anticipation, of the union that they would enjoy forever with God. The whole meal was thus both a prophetic symbol of the future and also a means of entering into that future in the present.[18]

The celebration of communion is supposed to be an appetizer, a foretaste of the perfect unity and healing we will experience in the coming kingdom.

I am reminded of a communion service in my church following a difficult conflict. Relationships were strained; divergent values and perspectives made living in community challenging. As we gathered before the table on Sunday, we were invited to come forward and tear a piece of bread from a single loaf, then walk across the sanctuary and share our bread with someone else—someone with whom we felt estranged because of the conflict. The purpose was not to solve our differences, but rather to acknowledge our unity in Christ despite our differences. It was a sign of commitment to one another. It not only required courage to reach out to a person who may have wounded you, it required humility to receive the bread as well. Uncomfortable? Definitely. Healing? Powerfully. Throughout the sanctuary our consumer values of comfort and homogeneity were crucified, and our ability to envision a new way of living together was kindled. That day the kingdom of God felt a little bit closer, and the church became a momentary refuge in a world of division.

Chapter 8

Around the Table

*Let us not forget … that our life is a pilgrim's
progress, and that we are strangers on the earth,
but that we have a God and Father who preserves
strangers, and that we are all brothers.*

Vincent van Gogh

Lonely Together

Turkey, mashed potatoes and gravy, cranberry sauce. The combination of morsels accumulating on my plastic tray should have been a clue, but my focus was elsewhere. As the only child in the cafeteria, I was mindful to keep a comfortable distance from the others in line as I scooted my tray along. Born and raised a suburbanite, my inherited suspicion of strangers was a value I accepted as perfectly reasonable — especially this day. Around me was a hodgepodge of rickety outpatients, hospital employees, and homeless people beneath layers of coats, sweaters, and hats they did not remove even while eating.

I finally reached the cashier at the end of the counter and pulled the wad of one dollar bills my mother had given me from my pocket, careful not to show my cash to whoever might be in line behind me. "Son, you don't have to pay," the cashier said.

"Why not?" I asked.

"It's Thanksgiving," he said. "Tonight dinner is free."

As I shuffled to an isolated table with my stuffing and pumpkin pie, I wondered how I could have possibly forgotten it was Thanksgiving. Of course, ten-year-old boys have the prerogative to ignore calendars, only giving them a glance when Christmas, their birthday, or summer vacation draws near. But I had an additional excuse.

A few weeks earlier my mother had removed me from my fourth-grade class to travel with her to northern Michigan where her father was dying. Every day we made the short trek from our motel through the snowed-in streets to the hospital. While my mother and grandmother stayed with my grandfather (we called him Dada), I found ways to occupy myself elsewhere in the hospital. In truth, my grandfather frightened me and always had.

He was an imposing figure from Norwegian stock with a bellowing operatic voice, and his fantastical stories of bombing runs over Europe in World War II calcified his mythic status in my imagination. This Viking was not from my 1980s-MTV-cola war world. Seeing his emaciated body in the hospital bed, toothless and blind, only added to my fear. If Dada could not scare death away, who could?

Picking at my Thanksgiving dinner in the cafeteria, I felt incredibly sad. I don't remember crying, but maybe I don't want to. Thanksgivings had always been a bountiful feast at my parents' house with aunts, uncles, cousins, and dogs gathered around the table covered with delectable dishes. But I was sitting alone, on a vinyl chair, under florescent hospital lights, looking on my tray for something edible, forget delectable. No one should be alone on Thanksgiving.

Of course I wasn't completely alone; there were people all around me. But sometimes the worst loneliness happens in a crowd. I shared that Thanksgiving meal with the rickety outpatients, hospital employees, and the homeless in their clothing cocoons. Words were never exchanged, eye contact was only made accidentally, but we were all bound together by a shared desire to be somewhere else. We were all lonely together.

Reflecting on the scene twenty years later, I wish I could go back and convince my ten-year-old self to not be afraid, to risk talking with someone, and maybe even join a table of other lonely souls in giving thanks. What stories might I have heard? What fascinating lessons might I have learned? What blessing might I have given to another? What divine light might have entered that hospital cafeteria if someone had found the courage to gather these ragtag dinner guests into a community of the broken? But no one found that courage. Like the broken bodies in the hospital beds on the floors above us, we ate our food in silence unaware of any suffering but our own.

THE POTATO EATERS

One of Vincent van Gogh's early works, *The Potato Eaters*, shows a peasant family gathered around a table. *(See color insert, Image 11.)* The darkness of the painting and earthiness of the characters was intentional. Van Gogh wanted the people to look like the dirty, dusty potatoes they were eating. Their hands have exaggerated knuckles almost simian in proportion. It's obvious that the same hands that dug the potatoes from the earth were now taking them from the bowl. The peasants have weathered faces with a look of exhaustion. Although they share the same table they seem disengaged—too weary from the labors of life to commune with each other.

The Potato Eaters was one of van Gogh's favorite paintings. Despite the depressing and dreary scene, van Gogh wanted to portray the dignity he saw in the peasants' existence. Within this dark composition Vincent painted hope. Above the table hangs a solitary lamp, its yellow flame illuminating the faces of the peasants with divine love. One is reminded of the ancient benediction:

> The LORD bless you and keep you;
> the LORD make his face to shine upon you and be gracious to you;
> the LORD lift up his countenance upon you and give you peace.[1]

Rather than a cathedral or church, van Gogh shows Christ's presence in a home, around a table, among ordinary people, in the most routine event of life. In addition to the lamp, the small round potatoes on the table resemble pieces of bread, and the man closest to the lamp is passing a cup to the woman beside him. Van Gogh is making the mundane gathering of lonely people around a sparse dinner table a sacred event. The moment is infused with the same significance and healing power as the Holy Eucharist, but this sacred meal is not served in a church or administered by clergy. Vincent declares Christ's presence with the poor even if the poor were not welcomed into the church.

Van Gogh's contempt for the institutional church was counterbalanced by his strong belief in the dignity and spiritual significance of ordinary life. "Whether an elderly man sitting by a fire, or peasants digging, sowing, and harvesting in the fields, or a simple frugal meal, van Gogh's depictions of peasants are often imbued with a numinous quality, a sense of the divine presence."[2] In *Starry Night* the golden light of the heavens, his color for divine love, is not seen in the church building. Instead, he reserves this sacred hue for the houses of his imaginary village. Each one is aglow with the life-giving warmth of God's presence. By placing the heavenly light in the humble cottages rather than the comparatively extravagant church, van Gogh visualizes the apostle Paul's belief that we have been given the treasure of God's light in ordinary "jars of clay, to show that the surpassing power belongs to God and not to us."[3]

Although *The Potato Eaters* was painted in the nineteenth century, if one imagines a change of décor in the room and the peasants' clothing, the painting could easily depict a contemporary household—each person encased in his or her own struggle, staring off into space and unable to be present with those around. Like the potato eaters, our modern consumer culture can form our lives into ones of quiet desperation, to use Thoreau's familiar term. We know the paradox of being simultaneously together and alone. Still, if Vincent's message is to be believed, there is hope. In the home, around the table, among a gathering of the lonely and the broken, the healing power of Christ's love may be found.

SOLITARY CONFINEMENT

Growing up in the suburbs has formed how I relate to others. We suburbanites, behind our store-bought façades, are extremely fearful and suspicious people. I've often wondered how my life and relationships would be different had I grown up on a farm or in a city. History and literature have shown that great heroes can emerge from the rugged life of the country, and the injustices of cities can produce tenacious and resilient spirits. But has anything so admirable ever emerged from the suburbs? The "burbs" were created to ease the stresses of both urban and rural life. But without these stresses, do the more admirable traits of human character remain dormant, and will prolonged exposure to the comforts of the suburbs cause emerging qualities to atrophy?

Suburban living began in the mid-twentieth century as a response to the congested and threatening conditions of cities. New neighborhoods were engineered outside the city, but still within driving distance, that guaranteed each family its own recreational space without sacrificing the benefits of urban living. Suburbs promised the best of both worlds—the convenience of the city with the space of the country. The driving value behind this design was comfort. But a century after the birth of suburban America, we have discovered that personal comfort and authentic community are often incongruous values. "The structure of the suburb tends to confine people to their houses and cars; it discourages strolling, walking, mingling with neighbors. The suburb is the last word in privatization, perhaps even its lethal consummation, and it spells the end of authentic civic life."[4]

It is no coincidence that the suburbs emerged during the same period consumerism became the dominant worldview in America. In many ways the suburb is the topological manifestation of consumerism, the ethos of commodification lived out in architectural form. Suburban living means dividing life into clearly discernable parts. Professional, recreational, industrial, and residential activities each have their zone. These zones are connected by roads where we drive alone in our cars, minivans, or SUVs. Socioeconomic zones are separated by neighborhoods and school districts. Family zones are demarcated by fences. And within the home, family members are zoned into private bedrooms—each with a television, Internet connection, and telephone. The suburb, like the consumer worldview from which it came, forms us to live fragmented and isolated lives of private consumption.

Philip Langdon, editor of *Progressive Architecture* magazine, says, "It is no coincidence that the moment when the United States has become a predominantly suburban nation, the country has suffered a bitter harvest of individualized trauma, family distress, and civic decay."[5] And James Howard Kunstler takes things a step further by saying the suburban way of life is "socially devastating and spiritually degrading."[6]

I have spent most of my life in the "socially devastating and spiritually degrading" suburbs, but it was the process of purchasing a house here that opened my eyes to the dehumanizing values around (and within) me. Over six months we must have toured a few hundred houses. Once I got past the shock of what I saw within other people's homes (honestly, no one is interested in buying a home that previously served as a shrine to Engelbert Humperdinck), I began to notice the common features of suburban houses. For example, most homes are set as far back from public spaces, the street and sidewalk, as possible. The rooms facing the street tend to be the spaces we use least—the formal living room or dining room. The spaces where real life happens, the kitchen and family room, are hidden in the back. Outdoor recreation is also confined to the back of the house, usually behind a fence. Everything about suburban home design communicates to the passerby, "Leave me alone!"

In his book *Following Christ in a Consumer Culture*, John Kavanaugh argues that our lifestyle of guarded isolation is the result of grounding our identities in external possessions. Consumerism has caused our attention to be fixated on the surface and style of our lives so that over time we have lost the ability to nourish our interior life. Kavanaugh says that without a meaningful interior life, a definable sense of self apart from possessions, we also lose the skills necessary to establish meaningful relationships. "We find that our ability to relate to other persons has atrophied. We know not how to give ourselves to the other since it is an empty fortress we call the self. And we know not how to receive the other's love, since one cannot love what one does not know."[7]

With the ability to relate meaningfully to others lost, the fully formed consumer is left only one path to seek fulfillment—consumption. Rather than framing one's identity around God, marriage, family, community, or any other system of relating, the consumer turns to commodified goods and experiences for self-definition. We construct a sense of self-identity through the purchases we make and the brands we display.

These two realities of consumer life—the inability to relate meaningfully to others and the formation of identity around stuff—explain our fearful suspicion of strangers. The person knocking at my door couldn't possibly be interested in me because I am not a person. In a consumer culture I am merely a set of possessions and preferences. I am a tall nonfat Earl Grey tea misto. I am a playlist on an iPod nano. I am a pair of customized Nikes. As the bumper sticker so sarcastically, but revealingly, states, "I shop therefore I am."

With no real sense of self apart from our possessions and preferences, every telephone ring, knock at the door, or alert from our inbox is not welcomed as a human-to-human connection, but merely an attempt to invade our personal zone to take some commodified part of "me" away. We instinctually assume that every stranger we meet has a hidden agenda. In our society it has become altogether implausible for anyone to be genuinely interested in us. The commodification of identity, and subsequent dehumanizing of individuals, has caused our present state of isolation and collective loneliness.

The popularity of blogs and social networking websites would seem to contradict this trend, but a more careful examination reveals the opposite. Lee Siegel, author of *Against the Machine: Being Human in the Age of the Electronic Mob*, says that we aren't actually interacting with real people online but "phantoms." The medium allows us to abandon real identities to become whoever we want, or whoever we think people want us to be. This can quickly deteriorate into "thuggish anonymity" when otherwise cordial people unleash brutal assaults on each other because the web cloaks their identity. The most famous example to date occurred when a thirteen-year-old girl committed suicide after being teased by a boy named Josh on MySpace. It was later discovered that Josh was not a real person, but the creation of a neighboring family.

Many people, myself included, use social networking sites as tools to keep in touch with people throughout the world, and for this purpose they are an incredible tool. But an increasing number of young people—as many as 250,000 new ones every day—use them to mediate nearly all of their personal interactions. Yet rather than encouraging healthy relationships with real people, these sites foster pseudo-relationships though shallow identities. Beyond demographic details like a person's age, gender, religion, or sexual orientation, a user's Facebook page reveals identity primarily through their consumer preferences: favorite music, favorite movies, favorite books, and favorite TV shows. Combined with photos and other carefully, or carelessly, selected materials, we are invited to present a "profile" to others that amounts to a digital façade. And by "friending" someone on the site we aren't actually committing to a relationship, but simply allowing them a closer look at our phantom consumer identity.

The appeal of social networking sites is the ability to simultaneously have hundreds of "friends" without actually risking the emotional investment of a real human relationship. As a result, relying on these sites for the bulk of one's relationships may exacerbate the aching loneliness we feel in our souls. If the suburb is the topographical expression of consumerism's dehumanizing effects, then Facebook is its digital counterpart.

SCUM OF THE EARTH

In first-century Judea, tax collectors were not well liked people. Have they ever been? Judea was under the control of the Roman Empire, and the Romans hired local Jews to collect taxes on their behalf. These tax collectors made a lucrative profit by taking more money than was required and pocketing the difference. This was Matthew's profession. He was essentially the Vito Corleone of Judea—the hoodlum who'd walk into your store and make you an offer you couldn't refuse. If you paid him, he'd leave you alone. If you didn't pay, he'd send his "friends" after you.

Despite Matthew's unsavory reputation, Jesus invited this scoundrel to follow him. Soon after, Matthew invited Jesus to his home for dinner. As the story goes, many more tax collectors and "sinners" came to eat with Jesus. Mark's account of the dinner party amplifies this detail by telling us these tax collectors and sinners were also followers of Jesus. It seems this syndicate of thieves and traitors were attracted to him. They found Jesus to be a desirable person to be with.

The religious leaders in Judea were appalled. They believed everyone had their proper place determined by wealth, heritage, or religious zeal. No "righteous" Jew would be caught dead associating with tax collectors. And, conversely, no tax collector would presume to share a table with a religious leader. After all, a stable society must maintain its zones and chastise those who ignore them. But these outcasts wanted to be with Jesus. To hell with societal norms and comfortable zones, they wanted a seat at his table. But why? What made this rabbi from Nazareth so attractive to these ne'er-do-wells?

The entire culture looked at the external realities of Matthew and his friends' lives and declared, "You are not acceptable. You have betrayed your countrymen and your heritage." They were not permitted into respectable Jewish society or the temple to worship God. But Jesus did not share this assessment. He did not screen people before allowing them into his life; he did not filter those who sent him a "friend request." He shared a table with tax collectors and sinners, thieves and prostitutes, and he did not expect them to change or verify their worthiness before doing so. Though he was a rabbi, a righteous teacher of the Law, he did not expect others to be like him before accepting them. Jesus' open, accepting, nonjudging presence made him outrageously attractive to people such as Matthew.

Unlike our suburban homes, the door to God's kingdom has no peephole. Unlike our Facebook profiles, God's kingdom has no filter. And unlike our consumer churches, God's kingdom has no target audience.

Jesus spoke about who was welcomed into the kingdom of God. He said, "Blessed are the poor in spirit, for theirs is the kingdom of heaven."[8] I like how Dallas Willard translates the verse. "Blessed are the spiritual zeros — the spiritually bankrupt, deprived and deficient, the spiritual beggars, those without a wisp of 'religion' — when the kingdom of the heavens comes upon them."[9] Jesus affirms and welcomes those who are completely lost morally, spiritually, and socially. They too may know his friendship and sit at his table. And they are blessed because they have the most to benefit from God's acceptance and friendship. Jesus declares that his kingdom is not for those who have life figured out, for those with a steady job, happy family, and a retirement account. The kingdom is for sinners, for alcoholics, for adulterers, for traitors, for thieves.

Unlike most religious leaders at the time, Jesus did not categorize Matthew and his friends. He did not view them as a demographic to be avoided and dismissed. They were more than tax collectors, more than wealthy hoodlums, more than political traitors, and more than immoral scoundrels. They were human beings, each possessing an identity, perhaps wounded and hurting, residing deeper than most people were willing to explore. Jesus bestowed dignity on Matthew's friends by joining them at the dinner table where he could engage in the most ordinary of activities —a meal. At the table Jesus would move beyond the external commodities and labels of their lives to engage their true identities. At the table he would do his divine work among them.

A few years ago I met a pastor named Mike. He shepherds a church in Denver called Scum of the Earth. (The name is taken from a term the apostle Paul uses to describe himself in 1 Corinthians 4, and few Christians have used ever since.) The first time I met Mike I asked him what kind of people come to his church. He replied, "We are a church for the right-brained and the left out." His congregation is a mix of homeless people, runaways, searching teenagers, artists, and others who never found acceptance in more conventional churches. Mike said that no matter who comes through the door of their church, even if they are considered the scum of the earth, they will never be treated like the scum of the earth.

Mike's community understands that Jesus does not have a scum filter; he was a scum magnate. The scum of the earth sought him out, and he was pleased to collect them into his new community of disciples—a community that did not judge, categorize, or label people based upon any external commodity. The ragtag army that followed Jesus through the Judean countryside defied and transcended every societal zone. And he assembled this wildly diverse group into a community that rejected the labels and categories of the culture. Jesus imagined a kingdom without zones, without barriers, and without peepholes. A kingdom where the lost, broken, and hurting are welcome just as they are. A kingdom where all are invited to recline at the table and where the Master will wait on them. By welcoming people like Matthew, Jesus was inaugurating a kingdom of divine hospitality.

TURKEY DINNER

We had been walking the streets of Tarsus for hours searching for the elusive home of Paul. Of course, every tourist guide clearly identified the location of St. Paul's Well, the supposed site of the apostle's ancient home, but the tangled web of streets was not easy to navigate. I was traveling in Turkey with a small group of college students. We had been staying near the university in Adana, about twenty-five miles from Tarsus. This day trip to visit Paul's home had been fueled by our interest in both the Bible and history.

Around dusk we finally stumbled upon it — the home of the man who wrote much of the New Testament, carried the gospel to Europe, and changed the course of world history. The site wasn't nearly as impressive as the man whose name it bore — just a few round stones behind an iron fence. To make matters worse, the nearby museum of antiquities that housed Roman artifacts had already closed. We mingled in the empty street debating our options while the temperature quickly dropped with the sun. We were cold, hungry, and disappointed.

Just then two young girls approached us. They were, like everyone else in Turkey, intrigued by one of my companions — a very tall African-American student who carried a basketball with him everywhere he went. He enjoyed being mistaken for Michael Jordan. The girls were sisters, perhaps ten and six years old, fairytale beautiful, with olive skin, black hair, and slate-blue eyes. The older sister spoke English and seemed delighted to practice her skill with real Americans. When we explained that we had come to visit St. Paul's home and the museum she told us not to leave, and then scurried off with her little sister.

When the girls finally returned they were not alone. Their entourage included parents, cousins, aunts, uncles, and neighbors — one of whom happened to be employed by the museum. He unlocked the door and the clan escorted us on a private tour of the museum. The warmth and kindness of the two girls and their family was astounding. Some of the students were suspicious, expecting our Turkish hosts to ask for some compensation for their services. But those concerns were forgotten once we finished the tour.

Outside once again, we thanked the family for their kindness. Our plan was to find a meal on the street, something mobile like kabobs, and get back to the bus station as quickly as possible. But when the family heard our plan they insisted we eat dinner at their home. A number of us politely declined in broken Turkish, but they stubbornly pretended not to hear us. One of the girls took my hand and grinned as she led me down the street.

It was a surreal experience. Ahead of me was my African-American friend, wearing headphones and juggling his basketball. He towered above the old man walking beside him, presumably the girls' grandfather, with a long white mustache, baggy linen pants, and sandals. *This would never happen in America*, I thought. *A family inviting ten foreign strangers off the street home for dinner.* I was both confused and delighted. When we arrived at the home, a simple apartment, I realized the family was not particularly wealthy. They were certainly not wealthy enough to feed ten Americans on a whim.

We were given seats around the dinner table while the women disappeared into the kitchen. The children, still fascinated by 3-D Americans, inspected our cameras, CD players, and clothing. The presence of ten foreign college students in their home didn't seem to affect the men who shouted at the soccer game on television. Then the food came. Lamb kabobs, flat bread, sweets, olives, tea and biscuits. Being extremely hungry from walking the streets of Tarsus, we received the food with genuine thanksgiving. While enjoying the feast I noticed only the Americans were eating. Then it occurred to me—the family had sacrificed their dinner for us.

At the table of that Muslim family in Turkey, I felt accepted and welcomed. No, I felt more than welcomed. I felt honored. Although a complete stranger and foreigner in their land, I was embraced, cared for, and given a place of honor in their home. This was the Christlike hospitality I had read about in the Scriptures but had never experienced in America. At that table in Tarsus, in the hometown of the apostle who commanded us to show hospitality to strangers,[10] I was given a glimpse of Christ's kingdom, a kingdom where all are welcomed into the household of God and given a seat at his table.

RULE 53, WHERE ARE YOU?

Long before hospitality was an industry dominated by hotels and restaurants, it was a way of life. The care I experienced in Tarsus, while foreign to me, has been practiced for thousands of years in the Middle East. In fact, Christians, Jews, and Muslims trace their practice of hospitality back to Abraham, the Old Testament patriarch and nomad.

According to Genesis 18, Abraham had been taking his usual midday siesta when he saw something strange. Coming toward his tent were three men. It was odd for anyone to be out in the heat of the day, so Abraham concluded these men must be travelers without a place to rest. He ran out to greet them, bowed to the ground, and respectfully called the leader "lord" (a common title offered to distinguished men). Abraham insisted the three enter his home to rest from their travels, then washed their dirty feet, had his wife prepare cakes, and roasted one of his finest calves for the visitors' meal. While the strangers ate, Abraham remained standing to care for their needs. How amazed Abraham must have been when he later discovered he was not entertaining strangers, but God himself.

Those who traveled through the harsh lands of the ancient Middle East depended upon the hospitality of strangers for survival. The nomadic Bedouins of today still endure the harshness of the desert through a culture of hospitality. Their notion of hospitality is profoundly simple: host first, ask questions later. Caring for a traveler was not dependent upon a person's identity, only their need. When Abraham greeted the strangers at his tent, he took this idea of Bedouin hospitality a step further. When the visitor is a person of equal social rank, the host merely rises. But Abraham went out to welcome the strangers (inferring their superior rank), and he bowed to the ground and addressed the leader as "lord." Unaware of the travelers' true identity, Abraham offers himself as their "servant" despite being a very wealthy man with servants of his own.

Abraham asked no questions; he expected no payment. He placed no conditions upon his hospitality. He merely welcomed these total strangers as honored guests worthy of his very best food, effort, and attention. Only after the three strangers had eaten and rested did Abraham engage them in conversation and discover their true divine identity.

Following Abraham's example, the Scriptures repeatedly demand God's people to show sacrificial hospitality to strangers. God commands his people to act fairly toward strangers (Exodus 22:21), provide food for them (Leviticus 19:10), and love them as one of their own (Leviticus 19:34). And in the New Testament three apostles write repeatedly about the importance of hospitality,[11] a word that can be literally translated "love for strangers." But it is Jesus himself who lifts the importance of hospitality to a divine imperative. While teaching his followers about the judgment that awaits them, he says:

> Then the King will say to those on his right, "Come, you who are blessed of my Father, inherit the kingdom prepared for you from the foundation of the world. For I was hungry and you gave me food, I was thirsty and you gave me drink, I was a stranger and you welcomed me.... Truly, I say to you, as you did it to one of the least of these my brothers, you did it to me."[12]

Christians in the monastic movement later codified the biblical ethic of hospitality as Benedictine Rule #53: "All guests who present themselves are to be welcomed as Christ, for he himself will say, 'I was a stranger and you welcomed me.'" The abbot of the monastery was expected to personally welcome guests and wash their feet. If the abbot was in a season of fasting, he would interrupt the fast to eat with the guest. Only after extending his warmest hospitality would the abbot engage in conversation with the stranger, learn his identity and story, and invite him into the ordinary life of the Christian community.

Hospitality was never about changing oneself to fit the desires and expectations of the guest, but rather about loving and honoring the guest by welcoming her into the reality of one's life and community with open arms. But this view has been radically changed in our consumer culture. Today, the goal of hospitality has become making the best possible impression upon a guest even if that impression is a false one. We do not wish for guests to see us as we really are, but as we wish we were. The goal is to keep their attention fixed on the commodified goods and experiences that form the façades of our lives.

The church has also abandoned the traditional language of loving strangers in favor of a new dialect. We call it being "seeker sensitive." This new mindset has taken the age-old Bedouin idea of hospitality (host first, ask questions later) and reversed it. Now the church tries to discover everything possible about its target guests, and then host according to predetermined expectations. Rather than focusing on loving the flesh-and-blood human being that is presented to us, we engineer an experience to be attractive to a hypothetical person predetermined by demographic research.

The popular book that illustrates this trend is *Inside the Mind of Unchurched Harry and Mary*, published in 1993 to disseminate the seeker methodology. Harry and Mary are not actual people, but caricatures of the type of people the church is hoping to attract—upper-middle class white professional suburbanites without any significant past church involvement. The book includes five chapters of things Harry and Mary demand from a church: "Gimme Some Space," "Gimme Creativity," "Gimme Something Good," "Gimme Something I Can Relate To," and "Gimme Something from the Heart."[13] The entitlement language reflects the consumer origin of the seeker methodology. It isn't focused on equipping Christians to love strangers, but equipping an institution to supply religious goods and services to church shoppers.

Seeker sensitivity is the well-intentioned attempt to translate the Christian's responsibility to love strangers upon an institution, but something vital gets lost in translation. We forget that institutions cannot love, and institutions cannot show hospitality. The best they can do is target market themselves effectively to imaginary people like Harry and Mary. But in the process the responsibility to love is no longer felt by individual members of the church because the music, sermon, and facility have all been test-engineered to do the job instead. This allows individuals to remain, like the Pharisees, within comfortable cloisters of homogeneity. At such a church the Lord may be among us in the form of a stranger, but we would never know it unless he filled out a response card.

This contemporary game of image management, target marketing, and outsourcing hospitality to institutions is not one Jesus played. He did not target a demographic, but loved whoever was standing in front of him at the moment. He did not go after untempled Harry and Mary, but engaged people of every class, race, gender, and region. Jesus shows us a different way of relating to our fellow human beings, one altogether different than consumerism's dehumanizing method.

In Jesus we see a man whose identity is not constructed from the external commodities of his life, but rooted in an unchanging self-awareness given to him by his Father—an identity announced from the heavens at his baptism: "This is my beloved Son." With this defined sense of self, Jesus was able to fearlessly engage everyone he encountered. He is able to accept people just as they are without ever changing who he is.

He attracts and welcomes sinners, prostitutes, tax collectors, thieves, and criminals, but he does this without becoming a sinner, prostitute, tax collector, thief, or criminal. He never pandered to people or sought their approval. In fact, it was Jesus' refusal to make himself look good that regularly stumped his disciples. When people were drawn to him because of his teaching or miracles, he would remind them of the uglier reality of his life. He told one would-be follower, "Foxes have holes, and birds of the air have nests, but the Son of Man has nowhere to lay his head."[14] And with a huge crowd surrounding him, Jesus made radical and uncomfortable statements about drinking his blood and eating his flesh. As a result, many of his disciples left him.[15] He seemed to be intentionally thinning the herd by teaching unpopular ideas. Jesus had no need to disguise the undesirable elements of his life in order to promote the more desirable ones. It was by living from the truth of his own identity that he was able to accept the true identity of others.

DOCTOR STRANGERLOVE

While reclining at the table in Matthew's house, enjoying his dinner with the scum of the earth, Jesus noticed the Pharisees had arrived. These religious leaders, masters of image management and experts in social demographics, peered through Matthew's gate at the festivities in the courtyard. Imagine what they saw. A lavish house, a large table filled with food and drink, the courtyard stirring with obnoxious people dancing, smoking, and laughing—behaving the way people do when good wine is abundant. And right in the middle of the revelry is Jesus, the notorious rabbi, reclining at the table and enjoying the party.

The Pharisees were appalled. Calling one of Jesus' disciples to the gate, they inquired with a disgusted tone. "Why does your teacher eat with tax collectors and 'sinners'?"[16] But it was not a disciple who replied. Jesus found the question important enough to answer it himself. "It is not the healthy who need a doctor, but the sick," he said.[17] The Pharisees saw a rabbi defiling himself among sinners. But with his response Jesus was trying to open their eyes to see something more—not a rabbi among sinners, but a doctor healing the sick. Somehow, by simply sharing a table with Matthew and his friends, Jesus was bringing healing.

The English word *hospitality* originates from the same Latin root as the word *hospital*. A hospital is literally a "home for strangers." Of course, it has come to mean a place of healing. There is a link between being welcomed and being healed, and the link is more than just etymological.

When we are loved and accepted for who we really are—the true self that resides behind the false consumer identities—and welcomed into the life of another person without conditions, it brings healing to our souls. The love of the world is always conditional. Every strata of our culture and every advertisement we encounter reminds us that our significance and acceptability is rooted in what we achieve, what we have, what we do, how we look, and how we perform. Our acceptability is always conditional, and every human soul carries the wounds of rejection from not meeting someone's standard. How terrible when that wound is inflicted by a parent, a spouse, a community, or a church. Rejection always leaves a wound—not a visible one, but a cut in our souls whose scar we may carry for the remainder of our lives.

Philo of Alexandria once said, "Be kind, because everyone you meet is fighting a great battle." We are all fighting a terrible battle to be loved, a battle to prove we are significant and acceptable. Some of us fight by moving from one relationship to the next seeking to heal a wound that will not mend. Others fight by purchasing bigger and better tokens of success. Men often seek acceptability through achievement, but by their absence at home they inadvertently wound their wives and children and the cycle continues. Those who are most weary of the battle give up by turning to drugs, alcohol, food, sex, or any other temporary pleasure to mask their pain. In this way the brokenness of their souls is manifested in their bodies.

But hospitality, real hospitality, can be a healing balm on these wounds. To be accepted and loved just as we are—isn't that what we long for? And to be welcomed into another's life without façades and falsehoods—isn't that what we really want? Such soul healing cannot be achieved by target marketing or preference surveys that reinforce the façades of consumerism. And a church that indirectly communicates who is welcomed into its homogeneous unit will be an ineffective spiritual hospital. No, this kind of healing hospitality is personal, human, and beyond the powers of church growth strategies. This is the healing that only Christ, and the community filled with his Spirit, can perform.

Jesus was not blind, and he certainly was not ignorant. He knew that his dinner companions at Matthew's house were not moral people. He knew the depravity of their lives even better than the Pharisees did. But he loved and welcomed them nonetheless. He offered these wounded souls a refuge from their battle. Such is the love of God. His love is not blind. He sees us as we truly are. He excavates the broken identity we've buried beneath a mountain of Gap denim and overpriced lattes, sees its filthy condition, and says, "Come, my child, sit down and eat. I have prepared a place for you." And the warm glow of Christ illuminates the faces of all who have gathered at his table for healing. And for the first time we see one another as we truly are. Not labels. Not categories. Not demographics. But as people fearfully and wonderfully made in the image of God.

Our homes are to be hospitals—refuges of healing radiating the light of heaven. And our dinner tables are to be operating tables—the place where broken souls are made whole again. In our churches people should find rest from their battle for acceptance and release from the lie that they are nothing more than the goods they possess. When we lower our defenses, when we remove our façades and our peepholes, and we begin to be truly present with one another—then the healing power of the gospel can begin its work.

CHAPTER 9

TEACHING THE WORLD TO SING

Christ labored for thirty years in a humble carpenter's
shop to fulfill God's will. And God wills that in imitation
of Christ, man should live and walk humbly on earth,
not reaching for the sky, but bowing to humble things,
learning from the Gospels to be meek and humble of heart.

Vincent van Gogh

THE REAL THING

When Bill Backer's transatlantic flight landed at Shannon Airport, Ireland, on January 18, 1971, his fellow passengers were fuming. The flight's intended destination was London, but fog at Heathrow forced the late diversion. Backer and the other passengers were required to share hotel rooms or sleep at the airport. Understandably, the jet-lagged and fatigued travelers were irritated and even belligerent with the airline's representatives.

The following morning Backer, a creative advertising director working for Coca-Cola, noticed a transformation. A number of the passengers who had been the most furious the previous night were now quite cordial. They were gathered in the airport café, laughing and swapping tales while drinking bottles of Coke. Backer had an epiphany. "I began to see a bottle of Coca-Cola as more than a drink," he recalls. The liquid refresher was "a tiny bit of commonality between all peoples, a universally liked formula that would help keep them company for a few minutes."[1]

The following day Backer met with two songwriters in London to write new radio spots for Coca-Cola. He revealed a paper napkin with a single line written on it, "I'd like to buy the world a Coke and keep it company." The resulting television commercial that debuted in July 1971 featured a cast of 200 young people from twenty countries standing on a grassy hill holding bottles of Coke and singing Backer's song:

> I'd like to teach the world to sing
> In perfect harmony
> I'd like to buy the world a Coke
> And keep it company
> It's the real thing.

The song became an international hit, reaching #1 in the U.K. and #7 on U.S. charts. The television ad is still considered one of the most memorable commercials of all time.

By the 1970s Coca-Cola was already an internationally recognized brand, but Backer's song helped catapult the soft drink's image even higher. The scene of racial and cultural harmony on the hilltop communicated the scope of Coke's aspirations. The simple concoction of soda water, sugar, and caramel coloring would inaugurate what no one had ever accomplished — world peace. The grandiose, messianic overtone of the commercial is absurd on the surface, but it is remarkably consistent with Coke's corporate history.

Asa Candler purchased the formula for Coca-Cola from a pharmacist in 1887, and launched the Coca-Cola Company the following year with plans to aggressively market the drink. Candler was a devout Methodist from a revivalist background. He drew heavily from this experience when developing sales strategies for his new soda. He believed Coca-Cola's salesmen could convince the masses to embrace the soda if they possessed the same evangelical zeal and used the same tactics of persuasion as the old itinerant preachers who had crisscrossed the South.

Candler began a weeklong institute to indoctrinate his Coca-Cola sales force. One of the instructors told the salesmen to consider themselves like "the missionaries going into a foreign field" only carrying a secular religion. After completing the training, one of Candler's soda missionaries declared Coca-Cola to be "a thirst quenching, heaven-sent drink; a blessing to this sun-parched earth." Candler tapped his brother Warren Candler, a well known Methodist bishop, to begin the morning sales meetings with prayer, and he ended the week by leading the trainees in a stirring rendition of "Onward Christian Soldiers."[2]

Asa Chandler exploited his faith to do more than motivate his salesmen. He unashamedly piggybacked on missionary work to carry his soda overseas. Bishop Warren Candler believed Cuba was an ideal mission field for the gospel. With his brother's help, he founded a Methodist mission school on the island. But Asa's motivation wasn't purely evangelical. "We may be sure that commercial currents will follow the channels which education opens and deepens," he said. "Herein our duty and our interest coincide."[3] Asa Candler quickly hired a wine merchant in Havana to be the country's first Coca-Cola wholesaler.

The mission begun by Candler to take Coca-Cola to the ends of the earth has succeeded by any measure. By 1990, seventeen billion cases of Coke were available in over 200 counties, and 80 percent of adolescents around the world recognized the Coke logo. That is a higher rate of recognition than the symbol of any global religion. Even more remarkably, in most developing countries Coca-Cola is now more accessible and more affordable than clean drinking water. This fulfills a prophecy issued by Coke's former president, Robert Goizueta, in 1986:

> Right now, in the United States, people consume more soft drinks than any other liquid — including ordinary tap water. If we take full advantage of our opportunities, someday, not too many years into our second century, we will see the same wave catching on in market after market, until, eventually, the number one beverage on Earth will be soft drinks — our soft drinks.[4]

Carrying on Asa Candler's tradition of deifying Coke by assigning the drink omnipotent qualities, Goizueta went on to say: "A billion minutes ago, Christianity appeared. A billion seconds ago, the Beatles changed music forever. *A billion Coca-Colas ago was yesterday morning.*"[5]

Since its incorporation in 1887, the Coca-Cola Company has used messianic zeal and evangelistic strategies to become the most recognized brand on the planet. And by the late twentieth century, evangelicals were eager to return the compliment.

A PASSION FOR GROWTH

The lights in the sanctuary dimmed as 4,000 pastors braced themselves to be among the first to experience Mel Gibson's film, *The Passion of the Christ.* Shunning traditional Hollywood distribution methods, Gibson was touring the nation's largest churches to market his movie directly to church leaders. As the music swelled, words appeared on the screen: "Perhaps the greatest outreach opportunity in 2,000 years." It's a good thing the megachurch provided stacks of tissue boxes at the auditorium's entrance. This news was so good it could bring tears to a pastor's eyes. Finally, after two millennia, the church would have an outreach tool as pervasive as *Star Wars*, as emotionally gripping as James Cameron's *Titanic*, and as relevant as *Harry Potter*. Thanks to Mel Gibson, Christ was going to reign in the cinema.

Mel Gibson's pitch to the pastors on his marketing tour was simple: *The Passion* has the potential to spiritually impact millions of people. If your church participates in marketing the film, the logic went, it will also reap the benefits. The strategy was the brainchild of Motive Marketing, the firm hired by Gibson to pitch his films to churches, and it worked brilliantly. *The Passion of the Christ* became the eighth largest grossing movie in history, pocketing over $600 million. Much of the credit for the financial success was attributed to the pastors and churches that put up *Passion* posters, preached *Passion* sermon series, rented whole theaters, and canvassed neighborhoods to promote the film.

Paul Lauer, president of Motive Marketing, says his company's primary mission isn't marketing movies, but rather "providing congregations with tools to further their goals." So, was *The Passion* the greatest opportunity for the church in 2,000 years? According to one researcher, as well as many congregations, it was not. The post-*Passion* research concluded, "Among the most startling outcomes ... is the apparent absence of a direct evangelistic impact by the movie.... Less than one-tenth of one percent of those who saw the film stated that they made a profession of faith or accepted Jesus Christ as their savior in reaction to the film's content."[6]

Based on these disappointing outcomes, one would think pastors would reject Disney's attempt at the same pitch two years later. But they didn't. In 2006, after witnessing Gibson rake in the returns, the Walt Disney Company hired Motive Marketing to promote its *Narnia* film to churches. Once again, churches rented theaters, members tacked up posters, and pastors preached *Narnia*-themed sermon series. Disney even sponsored a competition offering pastors who mentioned the film from the pulpit a chance to win a London vacation.

Motive Marketing is just one of many businesses capitalizing on the church's insatiable desire to make a big splash. Kingdom Ventures is a publicly traded company that makes a profit by helping smaller churches fulfill their desire to be big. From event planning and fundraising, to stocking sanctuaries with the latest multimedia technology and supplying vetted speakers and performance artists, Kingdom Ventures knows how to draw a crowd to church. In March 2003, after declaring a 285 percent growth in revenue, the company announced its new business model: "to become the driving force behind the growth of churches and other faith-based organizations."[7] Apparently the Spirit of God would be taking a supporting role.

All of this begs the question: Why is the church so susceptible to pitches and products promising big impact? Part of the answer lies with consumerism's bent toward sensationalism. Despite their overuse, advertisers will affirm that superlatives sell. Every business wants its product to be the "most prescribed," "most trusted," "most watched," or "best selling." These phrases all communicate the same thing to the buyer: *surely millions of people can't be wrong.* This message feeds into our broken, insecure human nature that longs for acceptability and being comfortably part of the crowd. As a result, in a consumer culture a product's perceived value is directly proportional to the number of people it impacts. Popularity not only equals success, it also equals legitimacy.

According to advertising expert James Twitchell, this is the genius behind the success of megachurches. "In old-time denominations," he says, "growth was not proof of value, stability was."[8] But in a consumer culture, that has radically changed. Today megachurches "concentrate on what makes the brand powerful: growth. What you sell is the perception that *whatever* it is that you are selling is in demand."[9] This helps explain why churches will repeatedly buy into plans promising big impact. The gospel and the church "selling" it cannot be legitimate if it is only "bought" by a select few. Continual growth and expanding impact are how we've come to define success. Among evangelical churches, growth has become both the goal *and* the product they're selling.

Pastors Tim Stevens and Tony Morgan outline this belief in their book, *Simply Strategic Growth.* In a chapter titled "Bigger Is Better," they write that "a church should always be bigger than it was. It should be constantly growing." And they "firmly believe that bigger is what God intended for his church. Consider Jesus' ministry on earth. Wherever he went, growing crowds gathered to hear what he had to say."[10] Stevens and Morgan seem to have forgotten that Jesus' earthly ministry ended with only a handful of followers remaining. Everyone else had either abandoned or betrayed him. By a strictly quantitative measure, Jesus' ministry was a failure. But that is a minor detail. What's most important is that a local church, like the consumer-capitalist culture around it, opens new markets, expands its impact, and grows continuously.

How could a church shaped by these values not be excited by a product promising to be the greatest growth opportunity in two millennia? Some might see *The Passion*'s marketing pitch as grandiose, but apparently most churches did not. It may be absurd to claim a soft drink can be the font of world peace, or for Volvo to say its cars "cannot only help save your life, but help save your soul as well," but the impact of Coca-Cola or Volvo ought to pale in comparison to the most legitimate and superlative product of all—God. Grandiosity is justifiable, even required, when you are selling the Almighty. After all, he *really is* the best.

IMPACT, MAN!

In 1990, a twenty-four year old computer animator named Phil Vischer sat in his Chicago apartment's spare bedroom working on his pet project —correction, his vegetable project. On his monitor a CG cucumber with expressive eyes and a single tooth grinned back at his creator. Phil Vischer had given life to what would become the bestselling line of Christian children's videos in history—VeggieTales.

Bob the Tomato and Larry the Cucumber became the mascots of Vischer's Christian animation studio, Big Idea Productions. As the business grew, Vischer recognized there was enormous interest in the clever storytelling, silly songs, and biblical values espoused by his troupe of Protestant produce. Before Big Idea, Christian entertainment for children was woefully behind the times. There was nothing to compete with the emerging world of music videos and cable television. But computer animation, now that was cutting-edge technology. VeggieTales was positioned to make a huge impact on children's entertainment.

Vischer believed that his "role here on earth was to dream up amazing things to do for God. If my dreams were selfless, God would make them all come true. My impact would be huge. The world would change."[11] When his evangelical desire for impact was finally paired with business strategies, Vischer was ready to compose a BHAG (Big Hairy Audacious Goal) for his studio. Big Idea's goal was "to be the most trusted of the top four family media brands within twenty years." As Vischer translated it, he wanted his company to become the "Christian Disney." To aim for anything less would be dishonoring to God. He explains:

> The Christians my grandparents admired—D. L. Moody, R. G. LeTourneau, Bill Bright—were fantastically enterprising. The Rock-

efellers of the Christian world. Occasionally I would read about different sorts of Christians that would confuse me, like, say, Mother Teresa. Mother Teresa seemed like a great woman, but her approach struck me as highly inefficient. I mean, she was literally feeding the poor. One at a time. Didn't she see that her impact would be much greater if she developed some sort of system for feeding the poor that could be franchised around the world? She could be the Ray Kroc of world hunger! Wouldn't that be better?[12]

Vischer set Big Idea on a course of rapid growth. By 1999, the company that had started with a smiling cucumber in Vischer's spare bedroom had grown to become the second largest producer of children's videos on the planet.

Then the bubble burst.

Big Idea's exponential growth had compromised the company's financial footing, expenses to produce its first feature film were skyrocketing, and a lawsuit filed by one of its video distributors was looming. Vischer's dream of building a Christian Disney that would impact the world for God was slipping through his fingers. As his company began to lay off employees and tighten its belt, Vischer began to question the belief system that had fueled his ministry aspirations:

God would never call us from greater impact to lesser impact! Impact is everything! How many kids did you invite to Sunday school? How many souls have you won? How big is your church? How many videos/records/books have you sold? How many people will be in heaven because of your efforts? Impact, man![13]

By 2003 the ride was over. Big Idea Productions filed for bankruptcy and was auctioned by the courts to the highest bidder. Vischer had lost his company and his dream. During Big Idea's postmortem, he dedicated a lot of time to reflection, prayer, and reading Scripture. What went wrong? Why had God killed his dream? During this season he questioned the authenticity of his own faith tradition. "The more I dove into Scripture, the more I realized I had been deluded. I had grown up drinking a dangerous cocktail—a mix of the gospel, the Protestant work ethic, and the American dream.... The Savior I was following seemed, in hindsight, equal parts Jesus, Ben Franklin, and Henry Ford. My eternal value was rooted in what I could accomplish."[14]

Phil Vischer's epiphany while scouring through the debris of his ministry was that the Christian life "wasn't about impact; it was about obedience."

THE DEFIANT ENTRY

Among beasts of burden, the donkey appears to be God's favorite. It was a donkey that carried Abraham and his son Isaac to the mountain where the first foreshadowing of Christ's atonement would play out. It was Balaam's donkey that recognized the presence of an angel standing in the road (while the prophet saw nothing) and from whose mouth God spoke his words. It was a donkey's jawbone that mighty Samson used to slay a thousand enemies. The Lord has employed donkeys to carry, to speak, and to kill, but one particularly blessed foal was used by God to defy the will of an entire nation.

There are only a handful of events from Jesus' life that are recorded by all four gospel writers. One is his celebratory entrance into Jerusalem riding a donkey. According to John's retelling, news that Jesus had raised Lazarus from the dead had spread rapidly from Bethany, the small town less than two miles east of Jerusalem. As the story was confirmed by eyewitnesses, one can imagine the hype that emerged among the subjugated Jews. *Is this God's promised deliverer? Has a new Moses come to save us from the oppression of Rome? Is he the divine king who will reign on David's throne in Jerusalem?*

It's likely that every move Jesus made in those days was closely watched and analyzed, everyone looking for affirmation that he really was the messiah. So when Jesus left Bethany on the road leading to Jerusalem one morning, people noticed. This was it — the confirmation they had been waiting for. Messengers ran ahead to Jerusalem, "Jesus, the prophet from Nazareth, the one who raised the dead man in Bethany, is coming!" The city was saturated with worshipers for Passover. They poured out of the gates and lined the road to catch a glimpse of their would-be king. The custom was common in the ancient world. When a king ventured off to war, his subjects streamed outside the city gates upon news from a herald of his imminent return. With shouts of adoration, they would celebrate his victorious homecoming and join his procession into the city where the king would resume his throne.

As Jesus drew closer to Jerusalem, the crowds began laying their cloaks on the road ahead of him and shouting "Hosanna!" a Hebrew word meaning "save us!" This is the scene as recorded by Mathew, Mark, and Luke, but the gospel of John adds an intriguing detail. The people also waved palm fronds as Jesus passed by. (This is why the day is remembered as Palm Sunday.) This seemingly insignificant observation is actually critical to understanding John's interpretation of the scene.

Less than two centuries before Christ, Judea was under Greco-Macedonian occupation. A Jewish revolt led by Judas Maccabee was successful at killing thousands of foreigners and retaking the temple in Jerusalem. The liberation was celebrated by waving palm fronds—a tradition that remains part of Hanukkah, the festival that commemorates the revolt. From that time the palm trees that covered the Jordan River valley became a symbol for the kingdom of Judea. In fact, the palm tree is still featured on the Israeli one-shekel coin today. Palms were the closest thing Jews had to a state flag. They were a symbol of national pride and power—the Judean stars and stripes.

By waving palms and shouting "save us!" the people were revealing their expectations of Jesus. They were celebrating the arrival of a divinely empowered ruler who would destroy the Romans and establish a new Jewish kingdom. He would repeat the liberation of Judas Maccabee but on a scale previously unheard of. After all, Jesus was powerful enough to raise the dead. The people were giddy with anticipation.

The nationalistic fervor of the people that Jesus' presence ignited was so big that his critics bemoaned, "The whole world has gone after him." If his greatest desire was to draw a crowd, he'd succeeded.

Cue the donkey.

According to John's account, after seeing the waving palms and hearing the shouts for political deliverance, "Jesus found a young donkey and sat on it."[15] This was his response to the people's desire—a donkey. The meaning of the gesture may not have been immediately obvious to the crowd. Even John admits that the disciples did not understand it at first, but later they recognized the act as the fulfillment of a prophecy from the Old Testament. Zechariah had foretold that the king would come to Jerusalem in gentleness and humility, riding on a donkey.[16] He would not be a violent liberator like Judas Maccabee. With his donkey, Jesus was symbolically rejecting the will of the people. Historians call this event Jesus' triumphant entry, but John's retelling might more accurately be called Jesus' defiant entry.

His refusal to pander to the crowd's desires inaugurated a week of defiance and rejection for Jesus. He entered Jerusalem and violently drove people out of the temple—not the Roman occupiers but Jewish merchants and traders. While teaching in the city, Jesus called the religious leaders hypocrites, blind guides, vipers, and children of hell. And to cap off a week that would have given any PR consultant a coronary, Jesus predicted the destruction of the temple—an immense cultural blasphemy of a proportion beyond our ability to fully understand. The mood of the city changed so dramatically that just days after welcoming Jesus with adoring shouts of "Hosanna!" the same crowd was now shouting, "Crucify him!" By the time of his execution on Friday, even Jesus' closest friends had abandoned him. A stranger was forced to help carry his cross.

Jesus wasn't driven by impact. His desire wasn't to attract an ever-increasing crowd of people. In fact, episodes like the events of Holy Week and his teaching to the crowds (John 6) reveal a Jesus who intentionally weeds out those who are attracted to him for the wrong reasons. Something as rudimentary as assembling a crowd was a goal far below his calling. Late-night television has proven that a man crushing beer cans on his forehead can draw a crowd. A two-liter of Diet Coke and a pack of Mentos mints can draw a crowd. For Jesus impact did not define legitimacy; bigger was not intrinsically better.

What compelled Jesus was not impact but obedience. He was nourished by doing everything his Father commanded. "My food is to do the will of him who sent me," he said.[17] Whether amid an adoring crowd entering Jerusalem, or isolated in the wilderness for forty days, Jesus' single-minded obedience to his Father never wavered. His legitimacy did not come from the size of the crowd he impacted, but from the One who declared from heaven, "This is my beloved Son with whom I am well pleased." With an identity anchored in his Father rather than his fans, Jesus was able to engage his mission and abandon the outcomes to God.

Of course, this did not mean he wasn't thinking about the impact of his mission or lacked a desire to reach all people with his love. Jesus' purpose *was* big, even cosmic in scope. "For God so loved the world (literally, 'cosmos') that he gave his only Son."[18] But the grandeur of Christ's mission stood in contrast with the humble strategy for its fulfillment. This is the paradox we, like his first disciples, often miss. In God's economy the smallest things have the biggest impact. Crowds are often wrong, donkeys are often blessed, and a rejected King conquers the world. As Jesus told his friends shortly after arriving in Jerusalem, "Truly, truly, I say to you, unless a grain of wheat falls into the earth and dies, it remains alone; but if it dies, it bears much fruit."[19]

Abandon the Outcomes

Over the course of his short career as an artist, van Gogh painted at least thirty canvases of sowers—simple peasants walking the fields and scattering seed. The sower represented the convergence of three of Vincent's passions: his regard for nature, his respect for peasants, and his love of the Bible. Agricultural metaphors were among the most common in Jesus' parables about the kingdom of God. When just twenty-four, Vincent heard a sermon about Jesus walking in a newly sown field that he said "made a deep impression on me."[20] The message also addressed the parable of the sower and the seeds, which helped Vincent frame his understanding of ministry.

Of particular interest to van Gogh was the passage from Mark's gospel in which Jesus compares God's kingdom to the mystery that exists between the sower's labor and the earth's produce. "The kingdom of God is as if a man should scatter seed on the ground. He sleeps and rises night and day, and the seed sprouts and grows; he knows not how. The earth produces by itself."[21] As a young pastor, Vincent described his work as sowing the Word of God like seed scattered on a field. His task was to faithfully throw the seed knowing the outcome was beyond his control.

These three loves — nature, peasants, and Scripture — explain why the sower is a persistent subject in van Gogh's portfolio, but it was Jean François Millet's famous painting that inspired Vincent's depiction. Millet's *Sower* of 1850 was a monumental painting in van Gogh's view. He was so captivated by Millet's depiction that he copied the figure in many of his own paintings. But Vincent's sowers differed from Millet's in one important aspect — scale.

Millet's work was forty inches high, and the sower filled the entire frame. Van Gogh's painting from 1888 is clearly modeled from Millet's work, but the sower neither fills the canvas nor dominates the composition. *(See color insert, Image 12.)* Instead, Vincent's painting is dominated by a radiant citron-yellow sun that saturates the sky with light. We know from his letters to his friends that van Gogh used yellow light and the sun to represent God. It is Christ who dominates his *Sower* painting, rather than the humble servant in the field.

The message of the composition is consistent with Vincent's own theology. The sower has a smaller, secondary part to play in a far larger mystery. The sower casts the seed upon the ground, and the seed sprouts, but he knows not how. The sower is neither the central player in this act of creation, nor is he the cause of the growth. The primary agent is God, and all that we sow and reap occurs under his sovereign eye. The sower cannot take responsibility for the results of his efforts; he can only play his part and abandon the outcomes to God.

This is a relevant message in our age of Consumer Christianity that is always looking for the next high-impact ministry. Van Gogh's painting reminds us that we have a role to play, but we are minor actors in a much larger cosmic drama. Our work certainly matters, but probably not as much as we'd like to think—because ultimately the outcome of our labor is not in our hands. We work, and the world is changed, but exactly how this spiritual impact occurs remains a mystery. This reality is illustrated by Jesus in the parable that impacted Vincent as a young man:

> A sower went out to sow. And as he sowed, some seeds fell along the path, and the birds came and devoured them. Other seeds fell on rocky ground, where they did not have much soil, and immediately they sprang up, since they had no depth of soil, but when the sun rose they were scorched. And since they had no root, they withered away. Other seeds fell among thorns, and the thorns grew up and choked them. Other seeds fell on good soil and produced grain, some a hundredfold, some sixty, some thirty. He who has ears, let him hear.[22]

Jesus goes on to interpret the story for his disciples. The seed is the word of the kingdom which people receive, but only some of the seed matures to produce grain.

This parable appears to have been in van Gogh's imagination when he painted his sower. His field includes a superfluous path or "rocky ground" as well as birds to snatch the seed away. And in the background, closest to the sun, is a field of mature grain ready for harvest. A variety of outcomes appears possible, but the sower is undeterred. He strides confidently forward—his task is to cast the seed whatever the result.

The agricultural vision of ministry presented by Jesus in the Gospels, full of mystery and mixed outcomes, is carried forward by the apostle Paul. Writing to the church in Corinth, Paul describes the Corinthians as "God's field." As the first person to preach the gospel in the city, Paul refers to himself as the sower—the one who "planted the seed." Apollos, his fellow servant of Christ, later came and watered it. "But God made it grow. So neither he who plants nor he who waters is anything, but only God who makes things grow."[23] Like van Gogh's painting, Paul recognizes God as the primary agent of growth. He is responsible for the outcomes, not the sower.

This is a perspective largely lost today. Rather than abandoning the outcomes to God, we've been formed to judge a ministry's legitimacy, and our own, based on measurable outcomes. The most common are referred to as the ABCs of ministry: attendance, buildings, and cash. If these three factors are increasing, we assume that our ministry is effective, our church is legitimate, and our community is blessed. But what if Jesus, Paul, and Vincent are right? What if the outcome of our labor is beyond our control? What if we are not the primary agents behind bountiful growth or its absence? What if we stopped judging ourselves and others based on outcomes which rightfully belong to God, and rediscovered the humility of the sower—the one who rises day and night, casts the seed upon the ground, and marvels as it grows?

THE DAISY CUTTER DOCTRINE

The pattern is predictable. A few thousand young church leaders gather at a warm climate resort for two and a half days to have a "life-changing ministry experience." They shuffle into the hotel's main ballroom, bags of complimentary goodies in hand, where their internal organs are realigned by the worship band's bass-thumping remix of "How Great Thou Art." After which the marquee speaker, usually a Baby Boomer ministry expert or large-church pastor, will fire up the audience with a call to "change the world for Christ," "impact a generation with the gospel," or "spark a revival in the church." Throughout the stump speech, the presenter will wax eloquent about the fate he or she foresees for the new generation of church leaders in the audience. "Your generation will do what mine could not." "The young leaders in the church are leading the way by throwing off what's come before." "You will be the generation to change the world." Convinced of their manifest destiny, the twentysomethings will head off to breakout sessions where they will learn the skills necessary to impact the world—usually from other twentysomethings.

I say the pattern is predictable because I've been to a fair number of ministry conferences, led my share of breakout sessions and, like most church leaders, I've gotten used to hearing the drumbeat of revolution. I call it the Daisy Cutter Doctrine: "Change the world through massive cultural upheaval and high-impact tactics." Daisy Cutter is the nickname of the largest nonnuclear bomb in the military's arsenal. In our age of laser-guided "smart" bombs, the Daisy Cutter isn't dropped to destroy targets anymore but to intimidate the enemy. When impact is more important than precision, there's nothing better than a 15,000-

pound Daisy Cutter for the mission. Likewise, the Daisy Cutter Doctrine is an approach to mission that values high impact and visibility above all else.

The shock-and-awe approach to mission is extremely appealing to people shaped by consumerism. It taps into our consumer-oriented desire for big impact and feeds the assumption that large equals legit. The psychological appeal is never explicit but always present: by making a huge impact you can convince the world of God's legitimacy as well as your own. That is an enticing promise particularly for younger leaders, many of whom have yet to establish their legitimacy and may have latent feelings of inadequacy.

But there is a less incriminating reason why we are attracted to the Daisy Cutter Doctrine—a big mission seems to logically demand a big strategy. Jesus has given his students an enormous task, "Go therefore and make disciples of all nations."[24] It's a mission that matches the scope of his own cosmic agenda. When Christians with a consumer consciousness try to wrap their imaginations around such a large undertaking, they will automatically think about products or corporations that have impacted the world and emulate the same methodologies. So we ask, How does Coca-Cola impact the world? How does Disney impact the world? How does Starbucks impact the world? And we forget to ask the only question that really matters: How does Jesus impact the world?

We have incorrectly made the scale of our methods conform to the scale of our mission. We have assumed that the magnitude of the ends should be proportional to the magnitude of the means. And in the process we've revealed how captivated our imaginations really are to consumerism. Gregory Boyd points out the error: "We are to transform the world. That's the call. But the *way* you do it from a kingdom perspective is very different from the way you do it from the world's perspective."[25] Failure to understand this has scarred the church throughout history. For example, through much of its history the church in Europe employed conventional (worldly) means to advance its spiritual mission. This resulted in the gospel being spread by the sword, and thus we now look back mournfully at the Crusades, the Inquisition, and the slaughter of native peoples in the Americas. Centuries removed from those atrocities, we wonder how people could do such things in the name of Christ. Did they not see how inconsistent those methods were with the ways of Jesus? At the time, of course, they did not.

Today we consider ourselves more enlightened, but are we? We may not use the sword to advance the church's mission anymore, but the sword is no longer the predominant instrument of cultural power and influence. Today the church emulates the methods of corporations and business, and many of us never pause to ask whether such tactics are consistent with the ways of Christ. Like the Crusaders, we seem content to leave such judgments for future generations with vision sharpened by history.

As Boyd said, the ways of the world differ from the ways of the kingdom. In the economy of God's kingdom, big does not beget big. It's precisely the opposite. The overwhelming message of Jesus' life and teaching is that small begets big. Consider: God's plan to redeem creation (big) is achieved through his incarnation as an impoverished baby (small). Jesus feeds thousands on a hillside (big) with just a few fish and loaves (small). Christ seeks to make disciples of all nations (big) but he starts with a handful of fishermen (small). Even Goliath (big) is defeated by David with a few stones (small).

This pattern is also repeated in Jesus' parables about the nature of his kingdom. He says, "The kingdom of heaven is like a grain of mustard seed that a man took and sowed in his field. It is the smallest of all seeds, but when it has grown it is larger than all the garden plants and becomes a tree, so that the birds of the air come and make nests in its branches."[26]

All of this affirms the counterintuitive nature of God's kingdom. The wisdom of God will not be grasped by those captivated by conventionality. It requires a far larger imagination. As Paul writes: "Has not God made foolish the wisdom of the world? ... God chose what is foolish in the world to shame the wise; God chose what is weak in the world to shame the strong; God chose what is low and despised in the world, even things that are not, to bring to nothing things that are, so that no human being might boast in the presence of God."[27]

Phil Vischer came to embrace the counterintuitive wisdom of God after losing his Daisy Cutter dream. He now advises other followers of Christ to embrace a mustard seed approach to changing the world:

> I am growing increasingly convinced that if every one of these kids burning with passion to write a hit Christian song or make that hit Christian movie or start that hit Christian ministry to change the world would instead focus their passion on walking with God on a daily basis, the world would change.... Because the world learns about God not by watching Christian movies, but by watching *Christians*.[28]

SOWING MUSTARD SEEDS

This book has not proposed new missional strategies. It has not advocated a new form of church organization, or the unfolding of an innovative program to reach a post-Christian culture. I have offered no grandiose prescription for revolution or ecclesiastical upheaval. These pages have contained no shock and awe, no scorched earth tactics, no Daisy Cutter Doctrine—perhaps to the reader's disappointment.

Instead, I have proposed that we respond to the overwhelming influence of consumerism by sowing seeds—silence, prayer, love, friendship, fasting, hospitality. These are not bombs to shake the world. They are not spectacular or popular. You won't see these listed among the strategies of Fortune 500 companies. These are grains of yeast that eventually work through the whole lump of dough. These are tiny and seemingly inconsequential mustard seeds that, when fully grown, become the largest plant in the garden. They are the practices and disciplines that can awaken our imaginations to the beauty and wonder of a divine kingdom that is increasingly difficult to perceive in a noisy world.

If we want to teach the world to sing, to help others experience the alternative life in the realm of God's loving rule, then we must first learn to carry the tune ourselves. Before we attempt to change institutions, or churches, or cultures we must change the way *we* think and perceive. The premise of this book has been that the Christian imagination must be free to sing a new song before the world can hear our music. This requires a process of deconstruction and reconstruction:

- Deconstructing our commodified view of God, and reconstructing a sense of wonder through silence.
- Deconstructing our branded identities, and reconstructing identities rooted in faith through love.
- Deconstructing our attempts at transformation through external events, and reconstructing internal transformation through prayer.
- Deconstructing our devotion to institutions as God's vessels, and reconstructing relationships with our brothers and sisters in Christ.
- Deconstructing our unceasing pursuit of pleasure, and reconstructing the redemptive power of suffering through fasting.
- Deconstructing our contentment with segregation, and reconstructing the unity of all people through the cross.
- Deconstructing the individualism pushed by consumerism, and reconstructing our love for strangers through hospitality.

All of this razing and building begins in our own imaginations. These are the seeds we are to sow in our own lives and in the communities we share life with. Of course, we must recognize that the sowing of these seeds will not guarantee a predictable outcome. After all, we are just sowers, the throwers of seed; God is the one who causes the growth. Seeing ourselves as secondary actors in a far larger drama, we discover the faith to surrender ourselves and our work to God who shines over all creation with his luminous love and omnipotent power. Dallas Willard says:

> The humble are dependent upon God, not on themselves. They humble themselves "under the mighty hand of God" (1 Peter 5:6).... They abandon outcomes entirely to him. They "cast all their anxieties upon him, because he cares for them" (vs. 7).... We do the very best we know, we work hard, and even self-sacrificially. But we do not carry the load.... In our love of Jesus and his Father, we truly have abandoned our life to him.[29]

EPILOGUE

I am still far from what I want to be, but with God's help I shall succeed. I want to be bound to Christ with unbreakable bonds and to feel these bonds.

Vincent van Gogh

I began this book on a lonely church balcony. I had escaped from the ministry conference because the high-tech extravaganza seemed to suck the oxygen out of my lungs, and I fled out the back as if the building were on fire. I turned my back on the dazzling platform, the lasers and screens, the drummer suspended from the ceiling. Outside I found peace, the stars appearing over the landscape drawing me back to God.

Like van Gogh more than a century ago, I've come to cherish the wonder of God in the created order around me and in the people beside me—sitting under the crabapple trees outside church as a kid, or visiting the children in the nursery before preaching a sermon today. This is often where I find God, but I lament his absence in many of the institutions and theatrical events that have taken his name. This church of Consumer Christianity is hauntingly illustrated in Ron English's painting of a franchised McChurch being straddled by King Kong. The consumer church may be radiating cultural relevancy, it may be exciting and fun, but it has lost its grip on me.

As night descended on the church balcony, I brought my questions to God. The questions were genuine. *Is this what Jesus envisioned? Is this why he came, and suffered, and died? Is this why he conquered death and evil, so that we might congregate for multimedia worship extravaganzas in his name?* I stayed on the balcony for twenty minutes, maybe thirty. I'm not sure—time seems different in silence. I thought seriously about leaving the church and the conference. I wanted to simply escape. But in my contemplation and prayer I discovered a secret, a secret that would not let me leave.

I returned to the auditorium. The spectacle was still underway. The band rocking, the drummer flailing on his perch, and the lasers beaming through the fog machines' vapor. But something was different. I was different. The combination of anger and sadness that had driven me from my seat and out to the balcony thirty minutes earlier was gone. In its place was what I can best describe as a holy indifference—a sense of detachment. I knew that what was happening *around* me didn't have power *over* me. Instead, my communion with Christ during the minutes on the balcony continued as if I were sitting in the eye of a hurricane. Thomas Kelly calls this experience "simultaneity."

There is a way of ordering our mental life on more than one level at once. On one level we may be thinking, discussing, seeing, calculating, meeting all the demands of external affairs. But deep within, behind the scenes, at a profounder level, we may also be in prayer and adoration, song and worship, and a gentle receptiveness to divine breathings.[1]

But this is not my secret. Holy indifference is not what led me back into the auditorium. In fact, it was precisely the opposite. It's another paradox of the spiritual life—the dual truth that nothing matters, and yet everything matters. On the balcony I found the tranquility I needed. I found the beauty and silence in which God's Spirit whispers. And I heard a secret that I had kept hidden from myself. Here is my secret—I am a Consumer Christian.

The anger and judgment that had driven me from the auditorium and onto that balcony was really about me. The spectacle had prompted such a visceral response because on the stage I saw a reflection of what was in my heart. On the balcony I had intended to point out the speck of consumerism in the church's eye, and God responded by pointing out the consumer plank in my own.

My secret is that I want to be relevant and popular. I want my desires fulfilled and pain minimized. I want a manageable relationship with an institution rather than messy relationships with real people. I want to be transformed into the image of Christ by showing up at entertaining events rather than through the hard work of discipline. I want to wear my faith on my sleeve and not look at the darkness in my heart. And above all, I want a controllable god. I want a divine commodity to do my will on earth as well as in heaven.

As these sobering truths settled upon me, I realized that leaving the church and the conference was not an option. I had to go back into the auditorium and face the truth about myself. This explains why the recommendations in this book have been primarily personal disciplines to awaken and transform, rather than calls for changes within the church. Silence, prayer, fasting, love, hospitality, and friendship—these are what I need to loosen consumerism's hold on me. And it is only when minds are illuminated, imaginations set free, and wounds healed, one by one, that real transformation can come to the church.

After preaching a sermon in which I spoke about consumerism's influence over us, a young man approached me at church. Mark wasn't American; he had emigrated a few years earlier. He asked if we could have lunch to talk. When we met later that week he asked me a simple question, "How do you do it?"

"How do I do what?" I asked.

"How do you see the problems in the church and still stick with it?" He went on to explain the nature of his problem. He was reacting to Consumer Christianity but didn't have the language to articulate the problem until hearing the sermon.

"I believe in God," he said, "but ever since coming to America my faith has been struggling. What I see around me isn't Christianity. It isn't what I read about Jesus in the Bible. I don't understand the church here. And now I'm even questioning God. If there is a God, why would he allow his church to behave this way?" Mark was ready to give up on the church and Christ. He returned to his original question. He wanted to know how I remain part of the church. "How do you do it?"

"*Why* I remain part of the church is easy to answer," I told him. "I remain because the church's struggle with consumerism is my own. I can't run away from the church anymore than I can run away from myself.

"*How* do I do it? That is a much more difficult question, and the answer takes some imagination. It begins with crabapple trees, children, and Vincent van Gogh."

Questions for Reflection and Conversation

Chapter 1: Slumber of the Imagination

Consider ...

... ways that you have seen Christians gain political and economic influence in our culture. How have you seen this influence used for good? How have you seen this influence abused?

... various Christian resources that you engage (radio, books, programs, church events). These resources probably communicate facts and truths, but how do they engage your imagination? What secular resources engage your imagination?

Imagine ...

... if Jesus was serious about the things he said in his Sermon on the Mount (read Matthew 5–7). Do you think it is really possible to love your enemies, to not be angry, to not judge others, and to live without lust? How would your life be different if these things are possible?

... a recent Christian teaching that you received through a sermon, small group, or book. Did the teaching result in any lasting impact on your behavior or life? Why do you think it is so hard for information, no matter how true it may be, to transform our lives?

Chapter 2: The Canvas of Silence

Consider ...

What role does silence have in your spiritual life? What does this reveal about your view of God?

How have you approached prayer and Scripture as a consumer? How have you alienated God?

Imagine ...

... a problem you are presently facing (physical, emotional, relational, professional, etc.). How would your perspective be different if you experienced the wonder of God amid your circumstances?

... something simple you can do to create silence in your life and open yourself to encounter the Infinite.

CHAPTER 3: BRANDING OF THE HEART

CONSIDER ...

... something you recently purchased because of its branding more than its quality. What do you value about this brand's identity? Why do you want your identity associated with it?

As a Christian, how are you focusing on the external elements of your religious life rather than on the transformation of your heart?

IMAGINE ...

... if all of our Christian-branded products and merchandise were gone. How would anyone know that you belong to Christ? What are the qualities that should mark the life of a Christian?

... if our Christian communities paid no attention to external appearances or labels. How would your church be different?

CHAPTER 4: AT ETERNITY'S GATE

CONSIDER ...

How do you evaluate whether or not a worship gathering was a "good" experience? How is this similar or different from the way you evaluate a nonreligious experience—a concert, movie, or theater event?

... a meaningful "mountaintop" event from your past. How did you encounter God there? What happened afterward?

IMAGINE ...

... if you lived in a part of the world where larger religious gatherings were outlawed. What impact would this have on your relationship with God? How would your Christian faith grow, and how would you encounter Christ?

... one way you can begin to experience God's presence in the ordinary activities of your life.

CHAPTER 5: WIND IN A BOTTLE

CONSIDER ...

How do you see churches cooperating with each other? How do you see churches competing with each other?

How does the idea of a truly omnipotent and uncontrollable God make you uncomfortable? Share a time when God didn't act the way you had predicted.

IMAGINE ...

Think of the people who have impacted your spiritual development most. How did you recognize the Spirit of Christ within them? If you could trade your engagement with institutions or programs for more of these kinds of relationships, would you?

... if the church valued fostering relationships with people more than building institutions and programs. How would the church and its mission look different?

CHAPTER 6: THE LAND OF DESIRE

CONSIDER ...

... an area of your life in which you are discontent. Is this discontentment the product of a legitimate need, or because you lack something you want? How can you know the difference?

... the areas of your life where you exhibit the least self-control. How does the consumer culture contribute to and reward your lack of self-control?

IMAGINE ...

... how your life and soul would be different if you were no longer exposed to 3,500 advertisements every day. Would anything about your life, self-identity, or relationships be *worse* without these advertisements?

... the rewards and joys promised by Christ to those who follow in his steps. How does this change your perspective on the things you suffer through in your present life circumstances?

CHAPTER 7: A REFUGE FOR MANY

CONSIDER ...

What do you think are legitimate and illegitimate reasons for leaving a church? How has individualism and personal preference impacted how we choose a spiritual community?

... a time you experienced conflict or discomfort as part of a community. How did you respond? Did you work through the problem within the community, or did you disengage and distance yourself from the community? What values influenced your response?

IMAGINE ...

... Henri Nouwen's description of a Christian community found on page 135. What would be more challenging about being in that kind of community? What would be most rewarding?

... someone on the periphery of your life or community. What is something you can do to welcome this person the way Christ welcomes you, and help him or her feel more included?

CHAPTER 8: AROUND THE TABLE

CONSIDER ...

... a time when you were part of a large group and still felt alone. Why is simply being with people not enough to cure our sense of loneliness?

... some of the labels used to identify people during the time of Jesus—Pharisee, Zealot, sinner, righteous. What labels do we use to identify people today, including those inside the church? What judgments are implied by each label?

IMAGINE ...

... the scene of Jesus at Matthew's house enjoying the party among the tax collectors and sinners. Change the scene to a contemporary setting—what kind of people might Jesus be found celebrating with today? What might be happening at the party? Would you ever engage with a community like that? Why or why not?

Recall a time when you were rejected by a person or community because you failed to meet a standard of acceptability. What wounds did this leave on your soul? Can you think of a time when you have been the one inflicting the wounds on another? How might life be different without those scars?

CHAPTER 9: TEACHING THE WORLD TO SING

CONSIDER ...

... the well-known Serenity Prayer: "God grant me the serenity to accept the things I cannot change; courage to change the things I can; and wisdom to know the difference." Is there a burden you carry that is beyond your power to change? How does van Gogh's *Sower* and Jesus' parable of the soils help us release these burdens?

... the popular Christian belief that "God would never call us from greater impact to lesser impact." Can you think of examples from the Bible, or your own experience, where moving from greater to lesser impact proved to be the *right* thing?

IMAGINE ...

Think of ways that you feel pressure to produce outcomes as a Christian — the expectations you feel from your church, family, or the larger Christian community. How did Jesus respond to people's expectations?

... if you truly abandoned the outcomes of your life to God. What would be different about how you live? Would you be more or less motivated to follow Christ?

NOTES

INTRODUCTION

1. Letter 164, in *The Complete Letters of Vincent van Gogh*, ed. Robert Harrison, trans. Johanna van Gogh-Bonger (New York: Bulfinch Press, 1991). Hereafter referred to as "Letter."
2. Letter 378.
3. Letter 543.
4. James Twitchell, *Shopping for God* (New York: Simon and Schuster, 2007), 20.
5. Thomas R. Kelly, *A Testament of Devotion* (New York: Harper, 1941), 33.

CHAPTER 1: SLUMBER OF THE IMAGINATION

1. Epcot film, Walt Disney, recorded October 27, 1966.
2. Pat Williams, *How to Be Like Walt* (Deerfield Beach, Fla.: HCI Books, 2004), 292.
3. P. J. O'Rourke, *Holidays in Hell* (New York: Grove Press, 2000), 184.
4. Christian Booksellers Association, highlights from the 2003 CBA convention, http://www.cbaonline.org/ (accessed December 15, 2006).
5. Stacy J. Willis, "The Passion of the Ca-Ching!," *Las Vegas Weekly*, February 26, 2004.
6. George Barna, *Think Like Jesus* (Nashville: Integrity, 2003), 40.
7. Ronald J. Sider, "The Scandal of the Evangelical Conscience," *Books and Culture*, January 1, 2005.
8. Rebecca Barnes and Lindy Lowry, "Special Report: The American Church in Crisis," *Outreach*, May/June 2006.
9. Walter Brueggemann, *The Prophetic Imagination*, 2nd ed. (Minneapolis: Fortress Press, 2001), 40.
10. Andy Stanley, "State of the Art," *Leadership* (Spring 2006).
11. Lyle E. Schaller, *The Very Large Church* (Nashville: Abingdon, 2000), 100.
12. Walter Brueggemann, *Interpretation and Obedience* (Minneapolis: Fortress Press, 1991), 199.
13. 1 Corinthians 13:11 NIV.
14. Matthew 19:14.
15. Matthew 18:3.
16. Mark 8:17–18.
17. Matthew 18:4.
18. Letter 425.
19. Letter B19.
20. Letter 531.

21. Letter 625.
22. Oswald Chambers, "February 10," in *My Utmost for His Highest* (Grand Rapids, Mich.: Discovery House, 1998).
23. Matthew 13:14.
24. Acts 7:56.
25. Letter 241.
26. Miyazaki Kentaro, "Hidden Christians in Contemporary Nagasaki," University of Wisconsin Oshkosh, http://www.uwosh.edu/faculty_staff/earns/miyazaki.html (accessed December 15, 2006).
27. "Japan's Crypto-Christians," *Time*, January 11, 1982.
28. Brueggemann, *The Prophetic Imagination*, 1.

CHAPTER 2: THE CANVAS OF SILENCE

1. Henri J. M. Nouwen, *The Way of the Heart: Desert Spirituality and Contemporary Ministry* (New York: Harper Collins, 1981), 45.
2. Ibid., 59.
3. Job 38:2–3.
4. Job 40:4.
5. Job 42:3.
6. "More People Use Christian Media Than Attend Church," *The Barna Update*, March 14, 2005, Barna.org. (accessed August 15, 2007).
7. David Van Biema, and Jeff Chu, "Does God Want You to Be Rich?" *Time*, September 10, 2006.
8. Jerry Falwell, "God Is Pro-War," *WorldNetDaily.com*, January 31, 2004 (accessed August 16, 2007).
9. Tony Jones, "Youth and Religion: An Interview with Christian Smith," 2005, Youth Specialties, http://www.youthspecialties.com/articles/topics/culture/smith.php (accessed April 21, 2008).
10. Hannah Elliot, "Prominent Professor Accused of Fraudulently Investing Millions," *Associated Baptist Press*, April 10, 2007.
11. David N. Bastian, "Reader's Forum: The Silenced Word," *Christianity Today*, March 5, 2001.
12. Letter 520.
13. Letter B7.
14. Letter 226.
15. Letter 242.
16. A. Sensier and P. Mantz, *Jean-Francois Millet: Peasant and Painter*, trans. H. de Kay (Cambridge, Mass.: J. R. Osgood, 1881), 120.
17. Romans 1:20.
18. Isaiah 55:8–9.
19. Leopold Stokowski, Leopold Stokowski Quotes, Thinkexist.com, http://www.thinkexist.com/quotes/leopold_stokowski/ (accessed April 21, 2008).

20. Mary T. Clark, *An Aquinas Reader* (Bronx, N.Y.: Fordham University Press, 2000), 12.

21. Eberhard Busch, *Karl Barth: His Life from Letters and Autobiographical Texts* (Minneapolis: Fortress Press, 1976), 489.

Chapter 3: Branding of the Heart

1. Damien Cave, "Air Jordans," Salon.com, August 5, 2002, http://dir.salon.com/story/ent/masterpiece/2002/08/05/air_jordan/index.html (accessed April 21, 2008).

2. Gary Wisby, "Police: Teen Admits Boy Was Killed for New Air Jordans," *Chicago Sun-Times*, April 4, 2005.

3. Rick Telander, "Your Sneakers or Your Life," *Sports Illustrated*, May 14, 1990.

4. "Study: Food in McDonald's Wrapper Tastes Better to Kids," August 6, 2007, CNN.com, http://www.cnn.com/2007/HEALTH/diet.fitness/08/06/mcdonalds.preschoolers.ap/index.html (accessed September 3, 2007).

5. Colin Bates, "Marketing Definitions: Brand," Building Brands, http://www.buildingbrands.com (accessed September 3, 2007).

6. Mercer Schudardt, "Swooshtika," *Regeneration Quarterly*, July 1, 1997.

7. "Study: Food in McDonald's Wrapper Tastes Better to Kids," CNN.com, August 6, 2007.

8. Bates, "Marketing Definitions: Brand."

9. Tom Beaudoin, *Consuming Faith* (Lanham, Md.: Sheed and Ward, 2003), 9.

10. Naomi Klein, *No Logo* (New York: Macmillan, 2000), 20.

11. Ibid., 21.

12. Geraldine E. Willigan, "High Performance Marketing: An Interview with Nike's Phil Knight," *Harvard Business Review* (July 1992), 92.

13. Klein, *No Logo*, 21.

14. Jean Baudrillard, *Jean Baudrillard: Selected Writings*, ed. Mark Poster, trans. Jacques Mourrain et al. (Palo Alto, Calif.: Stanford University Press, 2001), 49.

15. Steven Levy, "Finally, Vista Makes Its Debut, Now What?" *Newsweek*, February 3, 2007.

16. Schudardt, "Swooshtika."

17. Telander, "Your Sneakers or Your Life."

18. Caroline E. Meyer, "Nurturing Brand Loyalty: With Preschool Supplies, Firms Woo Future Customers — and Current Parents," *Washington Post*, October 12, 2003.

19. These are all actual names from Social Security records for the year 2000 as reported by Cleveland Evans.

20. Benjamin R. Barber, *Consumed* (New York: W. W. Norton and Co., 2007), 194.
21. Pete Ward, *Liquid Church* (Peabody, Mass.: Hendrickson, 2002), 64.
22. Douglas Atkin, *The Culting of Brands: When Customers Become True Believers* (New York: Portfolio, 2004), xi.
23. Ibid., 97.
24. Marty Neumeier, *The Brand Gap* (New York: AIGA, 2006), 41.
25. Mark Riddle, "Rant #2—The Christian Bookstore," TheOoze.com, April 11, 2002, http://www.theooze.com/articles/article.cfm?id=300&page1 (accessed June 6, 2006).
26. Ward, *Liquid Church*, 64.
27. Rick Warren, *The Purpose Driven Church* (Grand Rapids, Mich.: Zondervan, 1995), 280.
28. "Brand," http://www.1in3trinity.com/brand.html (accessed April 24, 2008).
29. "Fusing Faith into Fashion," http://www.1in3trinity.com/about.html (accessed April 24, 2008).
30. Dallas Willard, *The Divine Conspiracy* (San Francisco: HarperOne, 1998), 35–36.
31. Genesis 17:10–11.
32. Isaiah 52:1.
33. 1 Corinthians 7:19.
34. Philippians 3:5.
35. Romans 2; Galatians 5; 1 Corinthians 7.
36. Galatians 5:2.
37. Romans 2:29.
38. Deuteronomy 10:16; 30:6; Jeremiah 4:4.
39. Galatians 5:6.
40. Yes, these are all real products.
41. Colossians 3:12.
42. John 13:35.
43. *First Greek Life of Pachomius 4–5.*
44. "Iraq: Beneath the Bombings, Churches Are Growing," *Compass Direct News*, July 8, 2005, http://www.compassdirect.org (accessed September 20, 2007).
45. Luke 10:25–37.
46. Albert J. Lubin, *Stranger on the Earth: A Psychological Biography of Vincent van Gogh* (Cambridge, Mass.: Da Capo Press, 1996), 109–110.
47. Louis Pierard, *The Tragic Life of Vincent Van Gogh*, trans. Hebert Garland (London: J. Castle, 1925), 46.
48. Letter 226.
49. Letter 227.
50. Letter 121.
51. 1 Samuel 16:7.

CHAPTER 4: AT ETERNITY'S GATE

1. Letter 248.
2. Letter 334.
3. Joseph Pine and James H. Gilmore, *The Experience Economy: Work Is Theater and Every Business a Stage* (Cambridge, Mass.: Harvard Business School Press, 1999).
4. "No Experience Necessary," *Leadership Journal* (July 2001). Used with permission.
5. Perry Noble, "The Greatest Show on Earth," Out of Ur, December 18, 2006, http://www.blog.christianitytoday.com/outofur/archives/2006/12/the_greatest_sh.html (accessed October 1, 2007).
6. Ibid.
7. Tim Stevens and Tony Morgan, *Simply Strategic Growth: Attracting a Crowd to Your Church* (Loveland, Colo.: Group, 2005), 24.
8. Ibid., 37.
9. Ibid.
10. Ibid., 38.
11. Josiah C. Holland, "The Music of the Church," *Scribner's Monthly* 10 (1875).
12. Jeanne Halgren Kilde, *When Church Became Theater* (Oxford: Oxford University Press, 2002), 130.
13. Ibid., 215.
14. Ibid., 218.
15. Exodus 34:30.
16. 2 Corinthians 3:13.
17. Bob Smietana, "High-Tech Circuit Riders," *Christianity Today*, September, 2005.
18. *Exploring the Worship Spectrum*, ed. Paul A. Basden (Grand Rapids, Mich.: Zondervan, 2004).
19. 2 Corinthians 3:18.
20. John 4:21, 24.
21. Colossians 1:27 (italics added).
22. Sheldon Cheney, *Men Who Walked with God* (Whitefish, Mont.: Kessinger Publishing, 1997), 303.
23. 1 Thessalonians 5:17.
24. Brother Lawrence, "Words of Brother Lawrence," http://www.PracticeGodsPresence.com (accessed October 1, 2007).
25. Robert L. Thomas and Stanley N. Gundry, *A Harmony of the Gospels: New American Standard Bible* (New York: HarperCollins, 1986), 15.
26. E. Claude Gardner, "In Remembrance of Me," *Gospel Advocate*, June, 1998.
27. Gregory A. Boyd, interview by author, 7 November 2007.
28. "Barna Reviews Top Religious Trends of 2005," *The Barna Update*, December 20, 2005, Barna.org (accessed October 2, 2007).

29. Rick Richardson, *Experiencing Healing Prayer* (Downers Grove, Ill.: InterVarsity Press, 2005), 55.

30. Thomas à Kempis, *A Pattern for Life: Selected Writings of Thomas à Kempis* (Nashville: Upper Room Books, 1998), 52.

31. Ibid., 52–53.

CHAPTER 5: WIND IN A BOTTLE

1. "Royal Caribbean International Names Much-Anticipated Ultra Voyager," http://www.rclinvestor.com. Press release, November 9, 2004.

2. Lyle E. Schaller, *From Cooperation to Competition* (Nashville: Abingdon Press, 2006), 24.

3. Ibid., 51.

4. Ibid., 38.

5. There is a tragic irony about a court system that grants legal personhood to corporations but denies it for actual human beings prior to birth.

6. Benjamin R. Barber, *Consumed* (New York: W. W. Norton and Co., 2007), 175.

7. John 3:8.

8. Deuteronomy 6:5.

9. Tom Brown, "Jesus CEO," *Industry Week*, March 6, 1995.

10. Dallas Willard, "Living in the Vision of God," http://www.dwillard.org/articles/artview.asp?artID=96 (accessed November 30, 2007).

11. Letter 441.

12. Letter 531.

13. Letter 213.

14. Bill Hybels, "The Wake-Up Call of My Adult Life," from the Leadership Summit, August, 2007, Reveal, http://revealnow.com/story.asp?storyid=49. Online video. Accessed October 16, 2007.

15. Greg Hawkins, "Watch Greg Hawkins: Hear the Heart Behind REVEAL," Reveal, http://revealnow.com/story.asp?storyid=48. Online video. Accessed October 16, 2007.

16. Ibid.

17. Hybels, "The Wake-Up Call of My Adult Life."

18. Hawkins, "Watch Greg Hawkins: Hear the Heart Behind REVEAL."

19. Chris Armstrong, "The Future Lies in the Past," *Christianity Today*, February 2008.

CHAPTER 6: THE LAND OF DESIRE

1. Cited in Benjamin R. Barber, *Consumed* (New York: W. W. Norton and Co., 2007), 78.

2. Ibid., 178.

3. Cited in Rodney Clapp, "Why the Devil Takes VISA," *Christianity Today*, October 7, 1996.

4. James Twitchell, *Shopping for God* (New York: Simon and Schuster, 2007), 84.
5. Clapp, "Why the Devil Takes VISA."
6. John De Graaf ed., *Take Back Your Time* (San Francisco: Berrett-Koehler, 2003), 95.
7. George Barna, *Marketing the Church* (Colorado Springs: NavPress, 1988).
8. Ramin Setoodeh and Jennie Yabroff, "Princess Power," *Newsweek*, November 17, 2007.
9. Ibid.
10. Barber, *Consumed*, 20.
11. Joseph Epstein, "The Perpetual Adolescent," *The Weekly Standard*, vol. 9, no. 26 (March 2004).
12. Susan Samuelson, "Adventures in Agelessness," *Newsweek*, November 3, 2003.
13. M. Scott Peck, *The Road Less Traveled* (New York: Simon and Schuster, 1978), 19.
14. Gordon MacDonald, "So Many Infant Christians," October 1, 2007, *Leadership Journal*, http://www.outofur.com (accessed January 3, 2008).
15. 1 Corinthians 9:24–27.
16. 2 Peter 1:5–10.
17. C. S. Lewis, *The Weight of Glory* (New York: HarperCollins, 2001), 26.
18. Mark 10:21.
19. Isaiah 53:3–5.
20. Hebrews 12:2.
21. Letter 133.
22. Philippians 3:8.
23. Van Gogh's sermon, 5 November 1876, Letter 87.
24. Luke 22:42.
25. Philippians 2:8–10.
26. Letter B21.
27. Letter 218.
28. Dietrich Bonhoeffer, *The Cost of Discipleship* (New York: Simon and Schuster, 1995), 44.
29. James 1:2.
30. Dallas Willard, *The Divine Conspiracy* (San Francisco: HarperOne, 1998), 350.
31. Matthew 4:4.
32. Isaiah 55:1–3.

CHAPTER 7: A REFUGE FOR MANY

1. Saul Gonzales, "Cineplex Church," *Religion and Ethics Newsweekly*, May 31, 2002, no. 539.

2. Ibid.

3. Larry Osborne, "An Army of Ones," *Leadership Journal* (April 2005).

4. Rowland Croucher, "Church Growth and Pastoral Stress," John Mark Ministries, http://202.6.52.14/articles/9680.htm (accessed January 20, 2008).

5. 1 Corinthians 11:20–22.

6. Ken Dean, "Video Venues to the Rescue," *Church Executive*, September 2003.

7. Martin Gayford, *The Yellow House* (New York: Little, Brown and Co., 2006), 22.

8. Letter 544.

9. Letter 544a.

10. Cited in Gayford, *The Yellow House*, 247.

11. John 17:21.

12. Galatians 3:28.

13. Henri Nouwen, *Making All Things New* (San Francisco: HarperOne, 1981), 82.

14. Revelation 7:9.

15. Ephesians 2:15–16.

16. Colossians 3:11.

17. C. S. Lewis, *The Weight of Glory* (New York: HarperCollins, 2001), 26.

18. Paul Bradshaw, *Early Christian Worship* (Collegeville, Minn.: Liturgical Press, 1996), 40.

Chapter 8: Around the Table

1. Numbers 6:24–26.

2. Kathleen Powers Erickson, *At Eternity's Gate* (Grand Rapids, Mich.: Wm. B. Eerdmans, 1998), 86.

3. 2 Corinthians 4:7.

4. Andres Duany and Elizabeth Plater-Zyberk, "The Second Coming of the American Small Town," *Wilson Quarterly* (Winter 1992).

5. Philip Langdon, *A Better Place to Live: Reshaping the American Suburb* (Amherst, Mass.: University of Massachusetts Press, 1997), 1.

6. James Howard Kunstler, "Home from Nowhere," *The Atlantic Monthly*, September, 1996.

7. John F. Kavanaugh, *Still Following Christ in a Consumer Society* (Maryknoll, N.Y.: Orbis, 2000), 10.

8. Matthew 5:3.

9. Dallas Willard, *The Divine Conspiracy* (San Francisco: HarperOne, 1998), 100.

10. Romans 12:13.

11. Romans 12:13; Hebrews 13:2; 1 Peter 4:9; 3 John 5; 1 Timothy 3:2; Titus 1:8.

12. Matthew 25:34–36, 40.
13. Lee Strobel, *Inside the Mind of Unchurched Harry and Mary* (Grand Rapids, Mich.: Zondervan, 1993).
14. Matthew 8:20.
15. John 6:66.
16. Matthew 9:11 NIV.
17. Matthew 9:12 NIV.

CHAPTER 9: TEACHING THE WORLD TO SING

1. Bill Backer, *The Care and Feeding of Ideas* (New York: Times Books/Random House, 1993).
2. Mark Pendergrast, *For God, Country, and Coca-Cola: The Definitive History of the Great American Soft Drink and the Company That Makes It* (New York: Basic Books, 2000), 92.
3. Ibid., 94
4. Ibid., 367.
5. Ibid., 417.
6. George Barna, "New Survey Examines the Impact of Gibson's 'Passion' Movie," Barna Group, July 10, 2004, http://www.barna.org (accessed March 15, 2008).
7. "Kingdom Ventures Revenues Increase by 285% — Rapidly Growing Church Development Company Reports Strong Growth in Fiscal 2002," Business Wire, May 1, 2003, http://www.allbusiness.com (accessed March 15, 2008).
8. James Twitchell, *Shopping for God* (New York: Simon and Schuster, 2007), 282.
9. Ibid., 234.
10. Tim Stevens and Tony Morgan, *Simply Strategic Growth: Attracting a Crowd to Your Church* (Loveland, Colo.: Group, 2005), 193–194.
11. Phil Vischer, *Me, Myself, and Bob* (Nashville: Thomas Nelson, 2007), 237.
12. Ibid.
13. Ibid., 238.
14. Ibid., 237.
15. John 12:14.
16. Zechariah 9:9; John 12:14.
17. John 4:34.
18. John 3:16.
19. John 12:24.
20. Letter 101.
21. Mark 4:26–28.
22. Matthew 13:3–9.
23. 1 Corinthians 3:6–7 NIV.

24. Matthew 28:19.
25. Krista Tippett, "Evangelical Politics: 3 Generations," *Speaking of Faith*, April 17, 2008, http://www.speakingoffatih.publicradio.org. Radio broadcast.
26. Matthew 13:31–32.
27. 1 Corinthians 1:20, 27–29.
28. Vischer, *Me, Myself, and Bob*, 244.
29. Dallas Willard, "Living in the Vision of God," www.dwillard.org. http://dwillard.org/articles/artview.asp?artID=96 (accessed April 19, 2008).

EPILOGUE

1. Thomas R. Kelly, *A Testament of Devotion* (New York: Harper, 1941), 9.